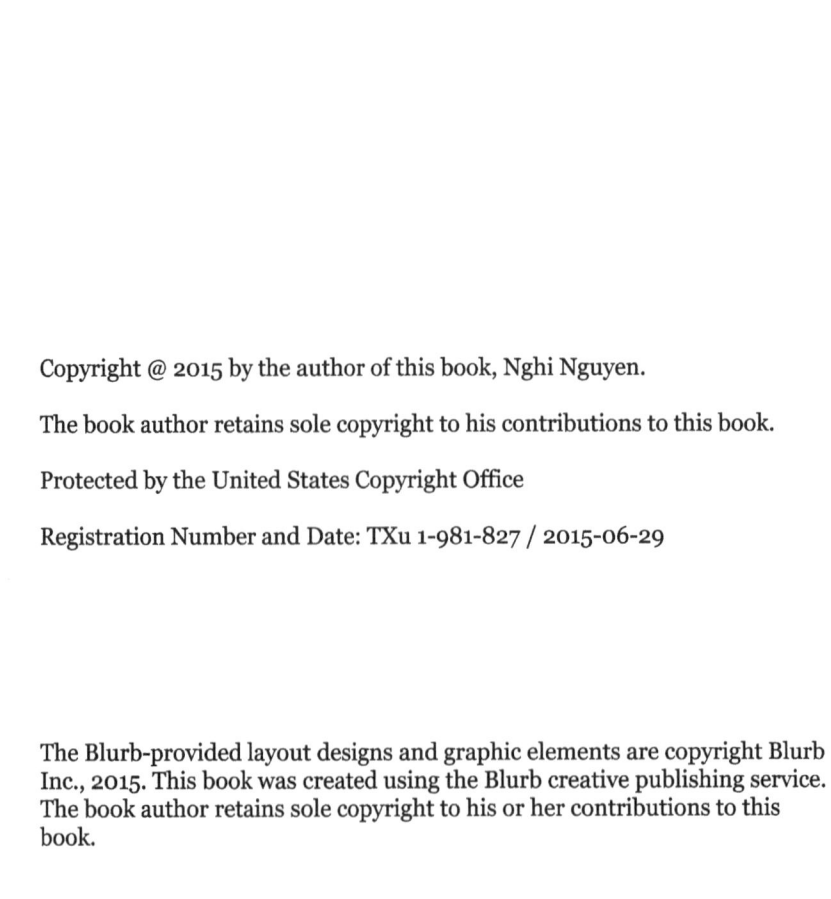

Copyright @ 2015 by the author of this book, Nghi Nguyen.

The book author retains sole copyright to his contributions to this book.

Protected by the United States Copyright Office

Registration Number and Date: TXu 1-981-827 / 2015-06-29

The Blurb-provided layout designs and graphic elements are copyright Blurb Inc., 2015. This book was created using the Blurb creative publishing service. The book author retains sole copyright to his or her contributions to this book.

For all my dearest friends....

This book is for you!

Contents

Introduction

Time
Loneliness Of The Passing Hours
Page 9

Music
Melodies of Love
Page 159

Dream
Living Out of Reality
Page 197

Index

About the Author

.......Introduction.......

Hello, and welcome to my ***A Collection of Heartbreak Love Poems*** book. This is Book 2 of my collections and is titled, ***Those Happy Days***.

Those Happy Days is one of my all-time favorite poems I've written over the years. Thus, I decided to use this poem as the title for this book.

Like Book 1, I do hope you enjoy reading these poems and hope, unlike the heartbreak exhibited in my poems, that you find true love and happiness in your life...

Thank you so much,

Nghi Nguyen

TIME
LONELINESS OF THE PASSING HOURS

Heartbreak Love Poems by NGHI NGUYEN

A Fool For You

I was a fool in love when you walked into my life.
You told me how much you loved me and how beautiful I looked.
You told me how you couldn't sleep when you closed your eyes because you kept on seeing my wonderful smile and lovely lips in your dreams.
I was a fool when you told me how much my love meant to you.
A fool I was to give you everything and to trust you, but how could I not love your words?
The words that praised me and made me cried.
When you told them to me they went through my heart.
I loved you with everything in life.
I was a doll, a puppet, and you were playing your lies on me.
The tears of laughter turned to the tears of pain when you told me you never loved me.
You never meant a single word you said.
Everything you said, they were all so wonderful, so dreadful, and so hard not to love.
Those lies, they're the killers of love.
A fool for you and a fool to have loved you so dearly.
Though you don't love me at all, I still love you.
I forget all the pain and tears you've given me because those words lifted me up and I was happy.

Time ~ Loneliness Of The Passing Hours

Acceptance of Love

When I fell in love with you I knew it wasn't going to be like what people said.
Some said love is hard and some said love is easy.
I didn't know the pain of loving someone until I met you.
Love came so sudden, but with you it was all I wanted.
Your love for me was all that I dreamed of from a lover.
You gave me tenderness and gave me all the passionate kisses when I wanted them, when I wanted love.
You loved me with all your heart, but when you walked away those kisses vanished with the air I breathed.
In the game of love I've learned to accept.
The acceptance of love, pain, tears, sorrows, and the heartbreaking moments when I'm without you.
In the game of love I've learned to accept the heartache and agony of losing someone I love so much.
Can you feel the pain inside me right now?
Do you still love me like you once did?
All the loving memories of love, pain and sorrow still remain inside me.
What are you feeling living without me in your arms?

Time ~ Loneliness Of The Passing Hours

Age Seventeen

I learned to love when I was seventeen.
I learned to love somebody like I had never before.
The one that taught me how to love was you.
You guided me through the sweet words and poems you dedicated to me.
I thought my first love would be complete but I was wrong.
I was too young to overcome my pain of losing you at seventeen.
I wanted to live long with you because you were so wonderful, so tender, and so beautiful to me.
Your words, and even your lies, kept me happy.
I didn't know what to do the day you left me.
I hung to the walls crying and remembering every last minute with you.
I looked into the mirror and asked why I was alone without you.
There was no one there to answer me.
I was seventeen and loving someone was too much for me.
Loving someone was great at first, but I didn't ask for pain and tears.
If only love was there for me when you broke me down.

All Out Of Tears

What is all this crying for?
Even if we both cry our love has gone and passed us by.
Loving is over, dreams are gone, and hopes are dead.
What is to cry for when tomorrow has come to an end?
The tears we've saved for all the heartbreak of those painful days in life have come.
They've washed away all the loving memories of the first day when life first blossomed with the growing seasons.
We're both out of tears, the tears for our lost love and the tears for our mistakes for all the pain we've put onto each other.
In time tears will have to dry out.
The time we've saved now has gone wasted along the roads that we both have shared.
It has gone wasted along the tracks that we both have walked on when you called me your love.

All The Nights Waiting

I knew things weren't going as well as I wanted.
I knew you no longer loved me like you used to, but I tried and tried.
I put away the pain in my heart and put away the tears when you were gone.
I wanted to give us another chance in love.
Facing you every day, the emptiness you gave me, the way you talked to me, how far and distance.
When you opened your mouth every word was wrong.
I longed for love and longed for you, but everyday things were falling apart.
You were getting farther and farther away in our love and my life.
It was so hard, but I put the pain away.
I wanted a bright future for us and wanted you to change, but you never did.
You never were the same in all those nights waiting for you.
I was waiting for your love in the dark empty bed.
I was waiting for tomorrow to come and for the sun to rise up to find you lying next to me on the bed.
But all the waiting was for nothing.
It didn't mean much to you, because you never wanted to love me like those days long gone by when love was still beautiful.

Alone Again With Love

Remembering the time we were together, they were the happiest moments in my life.
All that memories were so happy, but right now, there's nothing here.
I'm alone without you and with no one to talk to.
Can you see you've hurt me badly?
My love for you was true.
What's here to stay when you've left me?
Nights are cold without you and sometimes I just wish I had never met you so my heart won't be breaking right now.
Had I not met you then my dream wouldn't be dying today and I'd be happy without you here.
Had you not loved me the way you did I wouldn't have to fade away into the past to remember of those loving nights together.
Had you not spent those nights tightly and sweetly holding me I wouldn't be in pain today.
Now there's only an image of you and nothing else.
The love songs and the passing hours remind me of you.
Sometimes I just wish I had never met you before then today my heart couldn't be breaking and my dreams wouldn't be lost.
All alone I'd be happier knowing tomorrow will be a brighter day.

Alone

Alone, and where should I be?
Alone, and where's the love that I once had?
Lonely with no one but you on my mind.
Lonely knowing that all the tears I've saved for tomorrow now have come.
What's left in my life when you've gone?
I knew then life wouldn't be the same anymore when you said goodbye.
I knew my life would be different when you decided to walk out.
How many goodbyes?
How many more crying and falling tears before you change your mind and have a change of heart and return to me?
How many more hours spending right here wishing and hoping before you come and erase these burning tears?
I sit and count the passing hours.
If I have to sit here forever and count each passing seconds just to get your love back then the counting would be worth it.

Always The Last To Know

Smile to hide the pain deep in my heart.
Smile to hide the sorrows you've left me.
Winter comes and winter goes, but why is it so cold in my summer?
Why is it so dark in my love?
Is it just the way you left me here or is it just me still thinking about someone who never really loved me?
Leaves fall and leaves grow, and they change colors.
The smile comes and fakes away like those many seasons when I was always the last one to know when you'd come back and where you were going.
Your heart was so cold and your love was unkind to my empty heart.
I'm always waiting for you no matter what happens.
Even if the snow falls and covers up the world, I'll look for you under the cold wind.
I'll look for that smile and look for the happiness you once gave me because no matter what I do, I'll never be able to forget your love.

Another Day

I knew I was lying to myself and my heart all along.
I told myself you'd change and that you'd love me.
I lied to myself that you only hurt me because you loved me, but lies after lies I knew in my heart you didn't love me the way I wanted you to.
I loved you so much and didn't want to face the truth.
I didn't want to live with reality because it was killing me.
Reality was an arrow that shot through my heart.
You were the arrow and you pierced through my heart.
You left me crying but didn't care to know.
Maybe tomorrow you'll come and love me.
Another day in time, another moment in the future when you come and tell me how much you love me.
Tell me how much you've been keeping me in your heart and the love you have for me.
Another day when you say the word you love me.
That'll be the day I wait for.
I'm waiting and looking forward to those words that you'll give me.
Another day when the pain inside me turns to love and the tears of heartbreak are the tears of laughter with you.

Another Sad Goodbye

If you take my hands and ask me to go with you, how would I feel?
How would you feel deep inside?
Will I have to forget those sorrowful days living without you?
Will you love me all over again?
Will it starts all over?
I don't know if I'll laugh or cry, and don't know how I'd feel if you tell me that you've always loved me.
I want to believe and want to really love you all over again, but the pain of yesterday outlives the happiness of today.
I know it was just another sad goodbye and another mistake.
It was only one heartbreaking moment that you gave me, but whenever I think of it, my love for you just fades right away.
I want to hold and love you so much, but I just can't imagine you walking away again.
If you could've walked away for no reason once, you'll do it again.
I just feel that your love is a lit candle.
I don't know how long it'll stay lit, but it'll always go out when the time ends.
It'll be another say goodbye and another painful moment that I'd forever want to forget.
Just like the very first sad goodbye.

Another Try

I know our love wasn't perfect.
I know we didn't try our best to love each other, but I'm willing to take you back and love you with all my heart.
I just want you to come back and love me.
We can give our love another chance, just another try.
We can go back to those many happy days that we shared together.
If we just give it another try I know this time it'll work and we'll make it through.
Let's forget those days when we fought, when you walked away, and when I gave up on our love.
All we need is one more chance.
Just another try and we can both make it work this time.
We can love each other like we've never before.
The roads ahead of us are long so we shouldn't give up or fall down.
Just one more chance to love each other and this time I know we can go through and settle all the bad and ugly things.
We'll be happy and all it needs is for us to try and not give up in our love.

Baby Try

Try, baby, try, just to give us one more chance.
Try, baby, try, to go back to our loving days.
Our love has gone far from what we want it to be.
If you'd just try we can be together again.
All we need is a chance for our love to grow.
We've been waiting for all our lives to get through this, but if there isn't a chance, we won't get through it.
Forget the pain we had created for each other, close your eyes and forget every sad moments when we were together.
Let yourself be free, give us a chance and you'll see that it's worth trying.
If we only try to be lovers once again there'll be no regrets because our love will never be like it was before.
Don't give up on our love.
Love is to be here with us always, so baby, try again.
Don't give up on our days and chances because love is here forever with us.
Love will always be with you when you believe.
When life is empty forget about yesterday.
Put out your hands to me, give us a chance, and love is just here.
So don't worry and be here with me.

Back To You

I give back to you the roads of yesterday.
The roads we walked on when you took my hands into yours and told me how much my love meant to you.
Now I realize those loving words are all lies.
I give back to you the love you gave and give back to you everything from when our love did grow.
I gave my trust to you and gave myself into your caring arms.
Those caring arms that once held me so tight and with so much passion and tender, I thought you really cared but I was wrong.
You walked away faster than the falling rain and faster than my bleeding heart.
Now, everything has come, everything is put together pieces by pieces, lies by lies, and you've gone out of my life.
All the hatred and sad thoughts of us, which were once lovely thoughts, have now faded away with you.

Be A Man

Why do you have to hide?
Why do we have to play all these games?
Can you just look at me and tell me how much you care and love me?
I can't stand it anymore, why do you laugh when you see me?
Why do you talk sweet to me but can't tell me the truth in your heart?
I'm tired of seeing and watching you with someone else.
You're talking to this person while you stare at me, while you look with your lovely eyes.
You're just watching and staring with love at every move I make.
Be a man, be bold and tell me please.
Tell me your love and don't keep it all in your mind.
I want you and I love you too so don't be afraid to tell me that you also love me.
I won't turn you down and won't turn away from your love because I love you too much.
Be strong with your heart.
I love you when you look at me and when you smile, but it also hurts me to see you with someone else.
It hurts me when you're not telling me how much you truly feel inside.
I know you love me and want my love.
So you should know I also want your love in return.

Because There Was You

I remember every summer I spent with you.
I remember every summer kisses you put upon my lips when you left
while summer was still there and while the grass was still green.
The flowers were still fresh like that day when you decided all our loving memories spent together weren't good enough for you.
It was like when you decided the kisses you left on my lips weren't yours anymore.
When you were there with me I was so happy.
My life had never been so free and happy before you stepped into my world.
Your love kept me awake, it kept me living day by day, and when you weren't there, I began to die.
No regret at all in loving you.
Just feel sad now that you're not with me anymore.
Just the pain that you've left upon me today that makes me think of yesterday.

Time ~ Loneliness Of The Passing Hours

Before The Goodbye

Is it just me or has the world stopped turning?
Is it just me or has the happiness died away?
All the laughter that used to echo in the distance now has died.
All the laughter in my life now has faded away like the happy memories I used to have with you.
Is it just me or has the world stopped loving?
I have no one and no love.
Am I the only one in this silent world who's without love?
Should I just close my eyes and forget about love?
Should I just sleep away the pain you inflected on me and forever be happy with the false reality that I'm happy alone?
All the welcoming and all the goodbyes, they come and go like the rain outside.
They wash away the love and wash away the lies that are with your heart.
They wash away the hurtful memories when looking back on yesterday.
The memories that used to make me so happy.
What's left now?
What's there to think about?
No one here but the four walls.
No one cares anymore and no one is here at all but the goodbye of love.

Before The Night Takes You Away

One day you came and told me you had to go.
Silently, I looked at you with all my heart but couldn't find the right words to say.
I didn't know what you wanted to hear from me and didn't know what I wanted to hear from you.
I stood there in silent and watched in loneliness as you turned and walked away.
I wanted to reach out and hold you back but you slowly disappeared into the night.
I stood there thinking about tomorrow without you not knowing what I'd said or done to make you walk away.
I wondered if it was just you who wanted to go.
I wanted to make you happy and wanted things to be perfect always, but I couldn't be the one making all the things in this world as lovely as they could get.
You never shared your thoughts with me and never told me what you were thinking.
Maybe I was always the one who thought too much about us believing that we could be together forever.
In reality you were the one that was thinking of someone else.
I can't change the future and can't make you come back.
I can't say anything to change tomorrow because I know no matter what I say now you'd never come back.
You'll never come back and love me like you once promised you would.

Before The Sad Goodbye

I can hear the phone ringing but I'm too afraid to answer.
Maybe it's you on the line and you'll tell me you don't love me anymore.
Maybe this time you'll finally give up on our love and tell me goodbye.
Maybe tonight will be the final goodbye.
I don't want to be without you.
Can you hear my heart begging for your love and for you to stay?
Doesn't yesterday remind you of anything between us?
Can you still feel the love that was there or have you found someone else?
Someone who treats you much better than I can.
What else can I do to make you love me more?
I've given you everything and spent my whole life loving you more than anything.
What more can I give?
I have nothing left but this beating heart.
What more can I give when all that's left is this life?

Breathing For You

I saved all my energy for you and saved everything I had and owned.
They were all for you, but they weren't enough.
I gave you love and gave you my life.
Every minute away from you I never could take my mind off of you, but they weren't enough.
In the morning it was your face I wanted to see and no one else.
It was your laugh that I loved to hear over and over again.
I never could've known you weren't the one I'd live forever with.
I never could've known the end was coming before the music even ended.
Breathing for you, I breathed for your love and lived every second just to be happy with one person who'd care for me and who'd truly love me.
When I found you I thought you were that person, but I was wrong.
Every moment you laughed with me it was every little lies that you gave me.
How could I've known I was breathing for nothing when I fell into your arms?

Time ~ Loneliness Of The Passing Hours

Bring Those Days Back To Me

The day you left my heart went with you.
I couldn't go on living and couldn't close my eyes without thinking deeply about what you were doing and what you were thinking.
I never slept and never said a word.
I wasn't living the way I used to like when you were in my life.
Did you have to go and leve me here?
Why couldn't you just stay?
Why couldn't you tell me the reason why you had to go?
No matter what I do or say today, I'll never be able to get you back and hear you say you love me.
Bring those days back to me my sweet love.
Bring them back as if this world could go back to those wonderful and beautiful days when you kissed and held me in your arms.
Bring them back as if yesterday never did happen.
Come back to me like you always did every evening, when the door flew open and I could hear you laughing.
They were dreamy and lovely.
I want them back, I want you back, and I want you to bring those happy days back to me.

Broken Dreams

Would you be mad at me if I tell you I love you?
Would you be mad at me for telling you this so late?
Now, one way apart from each other, what can I tell you to make you happy?
What can I tell myself to let go of yesterday?
All the dreams we set for us are so long ago.
Tomorrow seems as if it was only seconds away, but it could ever be like that.
I look into your eyes and find nothing in return.
Those happy times are nothing more but sad memories waiting to be let go.
I see the rain falling and think for a moment it's really over between us.
I'm getting ready to let go of you and all the beautiful times together.
What more could I say to make you stay?
I was out of words to tell you.
The love has faded so what more could be said but goodbye?
Right at this moment, yesterday has passed by.
I could only turn around to look and hope that those memories will flash by and bring a smile to my face.
Whatever sad memories we had together I hope they'll die along with you and the passing seasons like those long dead dreams.

Time ~ Loneliness Of The Passing Hours

Broken Heart Never Sleeps

Many nights I haven't slept because of a broken heart.
Many nights I haven't dreamed because I've been crying for love.
I can still remember every whispering word the person has given me.
I haven't been able to sleep because I regret not holding on to love.
I cry nights and days because of loneliness.
I feel nothing but tears of heartbreak on my face.
I look at the mirror and cry to myself.
Many nights I wonder how regretful I am and how I want the person back with me.
Days I talk about my love and nights I cry about my love.
Broken hearted, I feel desperate and sorry for myself.
I don't want to sleep or eat just to end my misery of love.
Even if I fall asleep, I'd whisper my lover's name and cry about what has happened.
A broken heart never sleeps and my heart is broken.
I want nothing more but to keep on crying while telling myself to forget about love.
Soon my broken heart will heal, but I won't be able to sleep because a broken heart never sleeps.

By The Passing Hours

One time in your life when you someone "I Love You", and forever it sticks.
Forever, that phrase hurts you when you hear someone else says it.
When you told me tomorrow would be with us forever and told me you loved me, I believed you.
I took those three words inside my heart only to let them kill me slowly when I saw you with someone else.
The world collapsed before my eyes.
It was our beautiful world of tomorrow.
Tomorrow's here but there's only me,.
There's only one lonely heart waiting for you.
I wanted to be happy forever with you and every minute I wanted love to last forever.
For a moment love did seem to last forever until you said goodbye.
One word goodbye and all we had together faded with yesterday.
The broken dreams you gave me would always be for someone else and never for us.
My happiness deceived me and you lied through the pain.
All that we had together you'd given them to me but then the happiness you took away.
Now I sit by the passing hours hoping for you to come back with yesterday happiness like everything never really had happened.

Bye, Bye, Baby

Hold or kiss me one last time before we separate.
I've loved you always, but now, there's no more love for each other.
There's no more time for each other anymore.
We will be happier when we're apart because every minute that we spend together right now gives me no love but just tears.
Your love for me and my love for you, they're not here in our hearts anymore.
Maybe our love was just a game to play.
Bye, bye, baby, for you and I are no longer what we used to be.
We no longer love each other like those days of happiness.
We don't haveany time and sharing, or anything else period.
When we're together we just look at each other in dead silence.
The looking abd watching are giving up as time comes to an end for us.
Hold my hand baby for this will be the end of our love.

Can't See A Broken Heart

Did you care or even wanted to know what it felt like when you broke my heart?
You always ignored and hid away from what was there.
You never knew and didn't care what I was feeling and wondering when you broke my heart.
You just can't see a broken heart.
It's a bleeding heart that always breaks.
My life now is nothing but a wind that only survives during the winter.
You can't see the broken heart I'm keeping inside.
You've killed everything and hurt a beautiful heart that loved you.
What you've done will kill me and you know that for the best because you've broken my heart.
What do you expect a broken heart to do and what do you want me to do to satisfy you?
Why didn't you tell me you didn't love me?
Why play and fool around with a broken heart?
You can't see a broken heart when it hurts and can't touch the heart when it's dead.
I wish you just open up your life and feel love because there aren't enough hearts for you to break.
You might laugh at my broken heart and pain, but remember you just can't see a broken heart.

Close To My Heart

Close to my heart, I've always wanted to find someone who'd love me, treat me right, and care for me.
I want someone who I could spend my whole life with.
Close to my heart, I try to find this person whom I've never really found.
I meet someone and then fall in love, but in the end, this person never loves me.
There're only heartbreak and lies that make you happy at first and kill you in the end.
I don't know why it's so hard to find the right person.
Is it all pain and no love in my life?
Even if there's only pain I want to love and want to be loved by someone.
I'm tired and out of love, and all this searching has done me no good.
I've never found the right person for me.
Will I have to be alone in my life?
The roses have bloomed, but my heart has folded and refused to open.
Close to my heart, I always feel love is coming and feel tomorrow the right person will come and love me affectionately.
Yet, tomorrow has never come.
I'm here waiting and waiting, but just don't know when this person will arrive.
The roses are in love and they're blooming, but my heart is dead.
It has refused the warmth of the spring because of this awful loneliness.

Time ~ Loneliness Of The Passing Hours

Closer In Time

Don't cry for our love when it has died.
Don't think of me when you sit alone and don't call my name because it'll only bring back sad memories.
Let's move on and forget the past and live with the future.
Only this will make us happy and change our lives.
Forget the kisses you left on my lips when we kissed goodnight.
I won't remember and won't be thinking of your face when I'm alone.
You must do the same because thinking of yesterday will only bring pain and tears.
Closer in time maybe something will come upon us.
Maybe we'll both forget, maybe things will get better and then we can come back to each other.
For now, there's nothing we can do to fix this love that has been broken to pieces.
If you do find someone else, I'll be happy for you.
I won't be mad, but instead, I'll share the happiness you have with your new love.
If we're not meant to be then we shouldn't fight or go against our destiny.
In time, if there should be someone new in our lives we should both forget all the times we've spent together.
Just forget all the memories we've had because by forgetting we'll be happier in our new lives.

Cold Touch

Yesterday, I stood at the bridge watching the water in the lake flowing down the direction we walked home.
Yesterday, I stood at the bridge watching the sun go down like we used to before you were gone.
Yesterday, I stood alone without you, and today, I'm still without you.
Five years have passed since I last saw your face.
Days have passed by, winter came and autumn went by.
The touch in my hands; I've lost everything.
I can no longer feel or see you.
I can't feel the hands that once touched me so tenderly.
Those hands of love have disappeared like the warmth you gave me during those cold winter nights.
Time has passed by and things have changed.
Now, I stand here on this silent lonely bridge waiting for tomorrow while today is slowly dying away.
I'm waiting for today to end so I can come back tomorrow as the sun rises over the sky.
I'll be here again waiting for your love to come back to me on this lonely bridge.

Come Close To Me

Come close to me and tell me you'll be with me until the end of time.
Come close to me and tell me you still love me like you've had before.
Come close to me and say you'll be with me and will never let go no matter what happens.
You'll be with me and never let go of our love.
Please know that even if tomorrow when you leave me, we'll always be together in my heart.
Don't forget the last minute when we were together.
Don't forget the kiss when you knelled down and said you loved me.
Don't forget that tender moment.
Come close to me, come back and give me that kiss once again.
Our love is still tender like ever before.
Don't be sad when tomorrow we're both so far away from each other.
Come back to me, come close to me and whisper in my ears you want to be with me once again.

Come To Me

Let's celebrate this moment.
Laugh and cry with each other the tears of happiness because when the sun rises the happiness will end.
The loneliness of the past will once again come back, but I know I'll always wish and hope that you come back to ease this sorrow.
Life is full of happiness and unknowns.
I could only sit here and hope when the sun rises over the mountain your heart will break and it'll stay with me as you see the tears fall down my eyes.
I could only hope our love will bring us closer.
Let's live this moment like it'll never end and live this moment like we've never before.
Until tomorrow when you come back to me I'll smile with the pain.
When the sun shines down on me I hope you'll come back and smile with me.
When life once again belongs to us, our dreams will come back like ever before.

Courage To Say Goodbye

Everyone has the same heart and the same two hands.
Did you think I was made of stone?
Did you think I was metal?
I can feel pain and cry like everyone else.
Why must you always think you were more important than me?
You came in the silent of the night, filled me with love, and made me the happiest person on this Earth.
You made me feel safe like I had never felt before and you were the light in my life.
The trees and grass were green, but then again, everything was green when you were in my life.
Then you walked away and didn't have the courage to tell me the word goodbye.
You never had the courage to look me in the eyes and said that you had to go.
Why must you always think that I have a heart of stone?
You broke my heart to pieces when I found out you were gone.
There were those cold nights thinking of you while I couldn't sleep.
I awoke to find that you were no longer there.
You were one of my nightmares and were someone I desperately want to forget.
But how could I ever forget when so much love was given?

Crazy About You

Every day I sit behind you and can't stop but daydream about you.
I think about you, but you don't know.
I stare at you deeply in love, and when you step through the door, I look at you.
When you walk out the door I look for you.
Every day is the same over and over again.
Breakfast in the morning and I just smile and wonder what you're eating.
I look crazy, and maybe I am, because I'm crazy about you.
Morning arrives and I feel so happy because I get to see your beautiful face.
Lunchtime comes and I just wonder what you're doing.
Dinner time and I still think about what you're feeling at the moment.
I miss you when I don't see you before my eyes.
I love you when you're sitting in front of me.
So much love for you and so crazy about you.
You don't know what I'm feeling and how much as you walk with your love through the hallway.
You love someone else and don't know how my heart feels inside.
What I need, you just don't and will never know, because you never look at me when we're together.

Cry For Our Love

Yesterday, I cried for happiness and cried for our love.
Today, I cry for love and cry for the goodbye you've given me.
Time flies by so quickly that the tears now have almost gone dry in my eyes.
Your love is dry and dead like the day you walked off into the darkness.
Yesterday, I cried for happiness when we were still young and new to love.
We didn't know what love was and didn't know what the first kiss meant.
Then things changed and we began to love each other and had so much together.
There was so much happiness in our hands, yet, you still walked away.
Today, I cry for our love and cry the tears that used to be for happiness.
I cry the tears I saved for you to show how much you meant to me.
I cry to show you how much you've taken away from our love.
Tomorrow, even if you never come back and I never to see you again, I'll always remember the tears that I cried for you yesterday.
I'll always keep the tears I cry for you because they remind me of our love.

Curtain Close

When the curtain goes down it means the end has arrived.
When the curtain goes down and when I can no longer see the sun shining before my face, it means that your love for me has come to an end.
When the curtain goes down and when I can no longer see the stars shining down on me, it'd mean that you're gone.
I'll sit in this room and watch every car passes by as the lights shine through the curtains.
As each light flashes by I'll remember of you and our love.
The love, the lives, the beautiful minds, and the gorgeous eyes that looked at each other.
The lips that caress each other, were beautiful memories, but I'm here all alone.
When each light flashes against the curtain I'll turn on the radio and listen to the heartbreak songs.
I'll listen quietly while I remember of the dreams I had when I was with you.
The dreams I had of you and the love I had with you, everything by then will be sad.
It won't be the same like when I was with you and those dreams were so beautiful.

Days Of Loneliness

You told me you'd changed and promised you'd love me differently this time.
You said you couldn't live without me and so I took you back.
But it wasn't like I'd forgotten about you completely.
Days of waiting for you and nights of staring at the empty room.
I waited endlessly for you to say you were sorry so I could take you back and hold your love into my arms.
My heart blinded me when I believed you'd changed.
When we finally started over and just when things were back to normal, you once again left me broken hearted.
You left me with the same pain that was yesterday.
I was reliving those horrible memories right when we were starting over.
I didn't know whether it was you who hurt me more or it was my own foolish dreams with you that hurt more.
I told myself I'd never take you back, but my heart never worked with my mind no matter how badly you treated me.
I waited and waited for you again and again.
Maybe your love was more important than the pain itself, even if the love only lasted for a few special moments.

Deeply In Love

Blow out the candles like when you turned off the lights in our love.
Blow out the candles because it'll be the last time I'll ever see the lights shining in my fragile life.
Blow out the candles and let the night comes in.
Let the world knows how lonely my heart is.
How deeply in love I was with you and still very much so.
With all the heart I gave to you, I now sit here filled with loneliness.
Yet, you don't seem to care nor do you want to come and love me.
You no longer want to feel my gentle heart.
I was deeply in love with you because of the way you used to treat me when I was alone.
When my first love was torn apart, you were there for me.
I was deeply in love with you because of the heart that you gave me when I cried for the sadness of my lonely life.
No one seems to care now, especially you, the one who knows me all so well.
No one seems to love me like you used to do.
So blow out the candles and let the nights fill my heart and let the stars cry with me tonight.

Did You See It Breaking?

When you first went for it, did you know my heart was breaking?
When you laughed at me, when you talked to me, and when you looked at me, did you see it coming?
All the pain and love we had were all I ever wanted.
They were the things that build a good relationship, but you killed them.
Did you see it breaking when you touched me and said 'I love you'?
Did you really love me or did you just wanted to break my heart?
I saw the lies from your heart.
When you touched me all I saw was a white line before my eyes.
You wanted to break my heart but did you feel sorry for what you'd done?
Are you happier now then you did before?
Are you living in happiness when I'm here breaking down?
You shattered me into pieces when you laughed at my pain.
You asked for forgiveness and I forgave you.
I gave you another chance, but in my heart you were never the same like when I first loved you.

Distance Between Us

When I close my eyes, I feel I'm very near to your love.
When I close my eyes, I feel you in front of me.
The distance between us is short, yet, when I open my eyes, I see and hear nothing of you.
We're close but somehow our hearts are far away and nothing in this world could keep us together.
While I think you're here with me, reality strikes and hits me hard telling me our love has gone to the end.
You're the sun while I'm the moon.
The distance between us is so far away that it's hard to say what's ahead for us in the future.
I sit and watch the minutes we'd spent together pass by rapidly and look at myself in the mirror.
Tomorrow is lonely and will be sad without you.
I'll grow old and die alone, but in my heart, I'll keep those days I'd spent with you forever.

Don't Cry For Our Love

The tears of yesterday were of love and happiness when you stepped into my life and took away the loneliness that filled my mind.
The happy moments we spent together were important to me.
The tears of today are of loss and sadness when you walked away carrying with you all the love you once gave me.
The happy moments now turn to sadness.
Don't cry for the love we once had when we told each other how beautiful life was.
I thought for once heartbreak would never come, but it has today.
Should I cry for our love?
Should I cry or smile when we see each again and you're with your new love while I'm still alone?
Time will fly by, but will I ever forget you?
Time will die rapidly on me, but will you ever know?
Will you ever care for me anymore?

Don't Forget Me

Tomorrow when you leave I'll carry your love and care with me through life.
Tomorrow when you walk away from this love, you'll never turn back to love me like you once did.
I shouldn't have loved you so much when we were together.
I couldn't have seen that you'd be bored with me when time went on.
I couldn't have seen that you'd be walking away when I needed you most.
I need you now like I always have and want those moments again with you.
The special moments like when you held me close and whispered in my ears how much you loved me.
When you said you wanted to spend a lifetime with me and only me.
I can't forget and hope you won't forget me when you're with your new love.
Don't forget me when the nights come or when the days fade away.
Don't forget that we've had almost a lifetime of memories together.

Don't Know What To Say

When I see you I just can't stop but love you.
When I hear you talk I just forget where I am and forget who you are.
When you touch me I completely forget my name and don't know who I am anymore.
You're so lovely, so tender and soft, and your love is the greatest I've ever received.
I love you so much, but do you really love me?
Do you feel the same way that I do?
I don't know what to say when you don't call me on the phone.
I can't think straight when you don't talk to me, when I'm with you, and when you aren't listening to me.
You always seem to be doing whatever you want and don't pay much attention to me.
You don't love me, or do you?
I want to believe that you love me, but I don't know what to believe and don't know what to say.
I'm always happy being with you because I'm always smiling and laughing.
When I'm alone I think about myself and about you.
I just don't know if you love me the same way that I love you, or maybe you just want to love me then break my heart.
I love you so much and hope you love me too.

Don't Let Go Of Time

Even if tomorrow won't go our way, please don't be sad and don't let go of time.
Hold on to time and remember of our love.
Keep our hearts close to one another.
Let our hearts live like we want to live, like we want to love.
Time will grow, darkness and daylight will come, and we'll be walking in the shadows of one another.
Time will let us be with each other.
Remembering of the love today and the days of tomorrow.
There may be many lies and lost times together, but we won't give in because the love of today won't be falling to pieces.
Our love will be like the stars in the sky.
We'll reach for them and save all the memories and tears of our love forever.
The love today will never die so let's just hold on to each other.
Let's hold on to time and love.
Share feelings with each other before tomorrow dies away.

Don't Let The Sun Go Up

When the sun rises tomorrow, a new day will come, but at this very moment I wish the sun never rises.
If the sun comes up I'll have to say goodbye to you and it's the one word I never thought would come between us.
We've said many goodbyes before, but this time it'll be the final goodbye.
It'll be the last word you'd ever say to me.
I wish the last word coming out of your mouth wasn't goodbye.
I could wish for you to stay, but the love has dried out so what more do I have for you to stay?
What more do I have to give you but my heart and soul?
But right now, they're not enough for you anymore.
Your heart has changed for a long time and I can't stop it from going where it wants to.
I can't stop you from doing anything anymore.
What I could do now is hope for the sun to never come up on the other side of the mountain.
I wish tomorrow never comes because tonight I'll be holding you for one last time.
I'll hold you close even though you don't really want my arms around you.
I don't know whose arms you'll be in tomorrow, but I guess you think you'll be happier with this person.
I can't stop you from walking away and can't stop the sun from rising on the horizon.
I could only wish for tonight to be the last happy moment in my life.
I'll be the last and final moment between us before the sun rises and takes you away forever.

Don't Say Goodbye

I can sit here all night and wait for you to come back.
I can sit here all my life and wait for you to tell me how much you love me.
I can sit here days and nights just to hear your footsteps coming into the room.
For just one moment with you I'm willing to wait forever.
I can stay awake forever just to look at your face.
I can forget about everything that's happening in this world.
Forget the sadness and pain this crazy world is giving me.
For just one moment to be with you again, I'd give everything in my life to see that it happens.
I want to see and hold you one more time before the candle fades away.
Just one moment to tell you the love I have for you.
Don't say goodbye and don't say you'll leave me like you did once before.
My heart can't take it and it can't handle the pain being without you.
Just one more time, one more love, and one more kiss then forever I can be happy with or without you.

Dying Love

I'm sitting here watching the sunset over the hills.
I'm lying on the grass that's so green and full of life.
I'm sitting here watching the evening goes by only to be reminded of our love.
Over the mountain the clouds are moving in and covering up the blue sky just like your love leaving me here wondering when you'll come back like those white clouds.
I sit and wish one day when the clouds come and when the sun rises from the distance, we'll sit together in each other's arms.
We'll watch the evening passes by, and that day, I'll give my love to yours.
I'll give my heart to your body and will love you forever.
Right now, I'm siting here watching the day goes by and remembering the one who has left.
Right now, I'm sitting and remembering one yesterday when the sun was still bright and when the rain meant nothing.
Right now, I'm wishing for a brighter tomorrow when you come back to love me.

Ease My Sorrows

When I looked at you with the tears in your eyes, you knew I loved you more than anything in this world to see you in pain.
Your tears proved the love you had for me, but were these tears really from your love or just your lies?
You didn't know and never really understood how important it was to be loved.
You didn't love me even though I gave you my life.
You walked away without saying goodbye and today I remember that moment, but do you remember our love?
I want you to come and ease my sorrows when I'm alone.
Come to love me when I'm sad and worried.
Come and ease my tears and pain.
You hurt me deeply when you left without telling me the truth about your love.
I still love you and just want your love like yesterday before all the heartache.
You said you'd love me and would never leave, but now, where are you?
I'm here without your love and heart.
I'll never be sadder than this moment living without your love and tender.

Easy To Say Goodbye

It's easy for you to say goodbye when you don't know what love is and when you love someone without all your heart.
When you say the word love, you don't mean it.
You say love but you don't have any to give.
It's not easy for me to say goodbye when I have loved someone.
When I'm in love I want that person to return that love to me.
I want that person to respect me and feel my pain when I'm alone.
When I'm in love, I want to spend the rest of my life with that person.
For you, love is just a game and when you're bored, you just run off.
Love for me is a treasure because it's hard to find.
I cherish love and don't play around with it.
When I do love, I don't play with the people's heart.
When I love someone I love with all my heart and soul.
I'm not like you because when you fall in love, you only want the tender moments and then leave behind tears.
Love is not that easy.
It hurts to understand, but for you, love is easy to walk away because you have no real love.

Time ~ Loneliness Of The Passing Hours

Emptiness

Now, face to face, we just look at each other like we've never known one another before.
Now, face to face, we just look in empty space trying to find the right words to say without hurting each other.
Now, face to face, our hearts seem to have letting go of those happy days.
We used to kiss when we were together, but the tenderness of those many kisses have faded away on our lips.
That closeness when you held me and when I touched you, they seem to have disappeared like the passing wind in those quiet nights when I was without you.
The warmth of your hands isno longer there when you touch me and I just can't feel the love.
I don't feel the love that was once there when you really loved me with all your heart.
The love in your heart, it's no longer there like it used to when you told me tomorrow belongs to us.
Now, sitting here facing each other, we wait for the hours to pass by because we no longer feel the same like those many times when love was still there for us.
The love is gone and all there's here is a river of emptiness.

Enough Pain In Loving You

I know that you hurt me badly and know that when I'm beside you, you don't love or do you care for me.
Yet, when you're in my life there's a happy smile on my face.
I know the love I give means nothing to you.
In return for my love, you only give me the falling tears and only want to treat me coldly.
But if that makes you feel good, and that being next to you makes me happy, I'm willing to sacrifice.
I know there's already enough pain in loving you, but when I'm away from you, every second and every minute, they hurt more than the tears you give when . you're beside me.
The pain is worth taking just to have you beside my broken heart.
As long as you're beside me I'll be happy.
I'll give everything just to be near you even if you never say you love me.
There's enough pain in love you, but without you, there's even more pain I'd have to deal with.
I would rather have all the pain of loveing you than to not have you at all.

Faded Love

Love was like a dream when I had you in my arms.
When we kissed, my love blossomed into a spring flower.
I wanted to have a little more dream together because I thought we were meant to be together.
I dreamed of a peaceful and happy future with you, but you shattered my dream like broken glass.
You walked away from love and the future I hoped for.
You didn't care to look back and didn't care anymore about us.
You walked away with your new love leaving behind the emptiness.
Did you know life wasn't the same without you?
I couldn't see the day because the sun refused to rise and set, and the moon didn't shine anymore for me.
What's the meaning of love and all the vows?
Didn't you know them?
You walked away and never did understand for me.

Fading Footsteps

The bell is ringing and another day comes to an end, which alos means another day living without you.
The bell is ringing as the sun goes down and the night comes, and this will be another night without you.
Another day passes by and the footsteps of when you first walked into my house now disappear.
Let me forget the memories of yesterday like another scene from a movie when lovers say goodbye.
Let me forget the memories of you like a scene when lovers are heartbroken by the pain of love.
How many days and nights have I slept without you?
I don't really know, and maybe it's because I don't really want to remember.
Maybe remembering will only hurt more.
Remembering of you is to remember of those fading footsteps that hurt me deep inside because when I think of them thenI think about you.
I begin to cry for our lost love and broken hearts.
I've lost those footsteps just like I've lose you.

Falling In Love

When I first fell in love I wasn't happy but instead I was scared and nervous.
My first love was beautiful like a dream that came true.
I was scared of love because I didn't know what I'd do once my love ended.
I was afraid of the coming days when love finally would vanish away into the dark night.
From then on we'd be apart and I wouldn't be able to stop thinking about those eyes and the beautiful smile that had once captured my heart.
You love someone so much today and then the next you lose your love.
I was afraid of giving love because I'd have to learn the pain when my love says goodbye.
I didn't want to watch the morning go by and wonder about tomorrow because my love has left me heartbroken.
I tried not to think about heartbreak because our love was going strong.
But the day faded, the night darkened, and my love ended in the warmth of spring.
Today, I think and dream of falling in love again, but what will be around the corner?
Will love treat me right, or will it be another memory not worth holding on to?
Who can stop love from dying when the person has stopped loving you?
I know I can't stop my heart from breaking apart.
Love is sweet and romantic, but it turns sour and tearful when that sad day comes and you have to say goodbye even though you don't want to.

Final Goodbye

When the sun goes down, it'll be the end.
When the stars fade away, it'll be the last time we'll look at each other.
Deep down, while I lie in the silent ground, I'll look up and see your face.
I'll see the tears falling down on me and wonder where I'll be tomorrow.
Will we ever meet again?
We'll never really know, but for now, I know we have to say goodbye.
There'll be memories of me left behind, but soon, these memories will fade away.
I'll be the wind passing through your fingers.
Everyone will slowly forget, but for now, I hope you won't cry because I don't want this to be a sad goodbye.
Still, how can I stop you from crying when you know we'll never be able to see each other in the morning.
At night, the dinner table and bed will be without me.
We'll forever meet without seeing each other.
What will you do tomorrow without me?
What will I be doing?
Does anyone know?
Does anyone really know what will happen?

Forever Gone

Don't be sad because we're apart forever.
I know I'll keep the memories we've had together and cherish every minute in my heart.
I'll never let go of these memories.
Don't be sad because we've become the waves in the ocean slowly drifting away.
We're apart in time when only our love is blossoming.
We're the sky and cloud that never touch.
Just when we've begun to know more and learn about what we want and need, our love dies away with the spring.
Our love is forever gone, and we have a long road to go.
Don't worry though because I'll remember all the love we've shared.
I'll remember all the tender and loving moments we've given to each other.
I'll never forget you, and I hope you'll never forget me.
We're not destined to be together.
We have no way of connecting our love when we're like the water flowing away in two directions.

Forever Waiting

All the years together, I thought we would've shared enough, but when you walked away without saying goodbye, I knew I was wrong.
The laughter we shared, I thought there'd be a smile on your face when you think about it, but all I saw in your eyes was emptiness.
Looking at you I felt nothing between us.
You were far away from my heart with the way we stared at each other.
I wished with all my heart for an explanation of why you left me, but all I found was the silence.
All I had was the emptiness of love.
There was nothing of me in your heart.
I could wait forever for you to come back, but you'd never find me the same way.
You could never love me the same way.
The passion was dead and it could never come back no matter how much I wanted it to.

Forgetful

Tomorrow when you leave and walk away to a new life, will you be happy with the new person?
Will you live your new life and completely forget about me?
Will you love this person like when you loved me?
When you leave our love will die.
It'll leave my heart like the dark clouds that keep on moving in to cover up those times we were together.
When you say goodbye our love will disappear like the sun behind the clouds.
You'll become forgetful and forget about those days and months when we were together.
You'll forget me, forget how important you are in my life, and forget the loving minutes when you bent down and kissed me.
You'll forget the nights when we lit the fire and sat together listening to the sounds of our heartbeats.
The fire now slowly dies, and sooner or later, you'll be like this fire burning out and then I'll be all alone.
Even if the fire continues to burn bright, I'd be the only one watching it.
No more love and no more sounds of laughter.
Our love has died and our heartbeats have stopped.
You and I, we'll be forever apart.

Time ~ Loneliness Of The Passing Hours

Goodbye To Yesterday

I'm holding a pain inside my heart without anyone to hold and love.
Life seems lonely as I grow old alone day by day.
How could you forget the times and moments I brought happiness into your life?
How could you forget those days when we loved each other more than anything in this whole world?
Goodbye, goodbye to yesterday and goodybe to the one I've loved and longed for in those many nights of happiness.
Goodbye to the memories I've shared with the one I thought really loved me.
Goodbye to the one who I couldn't bear to lose.
Goodbye, goodbye to the roads I once walked on with the one I loved and who said she loved me.
Goodbye to love and goodbye to the one who I thought loved me with everything.
Goodbye, goodbye to the warmth of spring time.
Goodbye to yesterday memories that'll only be in my dreams from this moment forward.
Goodbye, goodbye.

Goodbye To You

I want to know when you'll come to me and want to know when you'll love me.
I need you to tell and show how much love you have in your heart for me.
Sometimes I want to forget everything and just fall into your arms.
I want to pretend there's only us and no one else, but the words I want to hear never come out of your mouth.
Will you ever tell me these words?
How long have we met?
How many days and nights have we spent together?
How long will I have to wait to hear your lovely praises?
Your words of 'I love you' and 'I want to marry you', when will I hear them?
Do you really love me?
Do you ever love me in your heart?
If you do, please tell me now or you'll never see me again.
Time is growing and I'm dying with the passing time.

Goodnight To Love

The lights have gone up outside in the dark silent roads and the voices have all died down.
The flashing headlights coming every few minutes as I remember of you when I hear footsteps walking toward me from behind.
The silence creeps up on me like a forgotten memory.
What wonderful memories I've had with you when we walked together in those nights of love.
We watched the moon go down and sat together under the stars waiting for the sun to rise.
Those memories, how could you expect me to forget and not think about you?
I hear a car coming and think if only you were here right now then it'd be great because we can hold each other and smile the night away.
How wonderful life would be to go home together and dream of tomorrow.
Think about the plans of tomorrow as we lie in bed forgetting about the silent roads outside.
But now I walk and think alone, and everything I do is with no one here next to me.
I can't ask you for love and can't ask you for a kiss because you'll never come back.
You'll never kiss me and I'll never hear you say goodnight or goodbye.
Goodnight my love, goodnight to you and I hope somewhere you hear me say goodnight to you.
Goodnight to love, goodnight to all the pain and memories you've left behind.
Goodnight my sweet and innocent love.

Happiness Gone By

It was a big mistake to let you go when I had you in my arms so tight and you were still in love with me.
Those days are now far and long ago that they don't seem to leave us a touching or memorable feeling.
Those days were the happiest in our lives.
Happiness came to our hands but we didn't save it, but at least you always tried.
I was the one who gave up on our love.
Was it my fault or was it yours that our love fell apart?
Though you tried to work it out, I knew it was going to be over sooner or later.
Happiness gone by our eyes, and days by days, our love was dying along the passing lonely minute without one another.

Time ~ Loneliness Of The Passing Hours

Happiness Through Tonight

Tonight, I sit and listen to the stories you've hidden in your heart for so many years.
The time we've spent apart has killed the happiness that once surrounded us.
After tonight, you'll once again leave me.
Time's so short, yet it moves so fast.
Soon the stars will fade away into the morning light and the moon will disappear before our eyes in the horizon.
At this moment, we'll know the end is here.
Day by day, I'll be waiting for your return.
One week, two months, five years; who knows how long I'll have to wait?
But the love you've given me and the happiness in my heart will keep the days to come without you lively.
Let's keep tonight our night, and let's laugh through the night, even though I might cry for the sad goodbye tomorrow.
Don't let the tears stop the happiness of the night.
Tomorrow, when you continue your journey, I'll be home waiting for the one who I love.
Distance away, you and I, we'll be in each other hearts and that'll keep our happiness alive.

Hate Or Love

How many kisses had you given me?
How many of them had you left upon my lips?
Now you turn away saying nothing and leaving me here wondering of the reasons you've left.
Is it hate or love when the telephone rings and I pick it up but you refuse to answer?
Is it hate or love when the hello that once sounded so sweet now sounds so cold?
Why is the hello of yesterday so much more tenderly than today?
The silence from you only causes more pain for me.
The love you gave me was real and we both wanted it.
The love, then, is the hate of today when the phone rings and I don't dare to touch it.
Is it hate or love when the door we walked through yesterday now closes on us?
It now leaves us on the opposite ends like the telephone itself.

Have You Really Walked Away?

The night comes while I sit here waiting for you to walk through the door.
The clock ticks while the rain falls gently outside, and there's no sound of your car pulling into the driveway.
The night comes as I wait to hear the voice I've loved for so many nights.
The cars pass by with their lights flickering and shining.
I sit and wonder where you are.
Are you coming back to this place where you used to stay or are you going somewhere new?
Have you really walked away or am I just thinking the worse of our love?
I haven't seen you for so long thus I wonder about.
What has happened to your heart?
The last time we spoke you told me you wanted some time to be alone.
Does that mean our love has come to an end?
Have you really walked away?
I sit here thinking about you.
I hear the laughter, and it sounds as though you are with your new love.
I'm here trying to laugh and be happy for you, but why do I hear the sobbing of a lonely bird?

Heart Of Pain

Love is like the wind that passes by and leaves nothing behind.
It passes through my heart and soul never letting me enjoy the sensation of being cared for by someone who truly loves me.
Why is my life always so desolate?
Why is love treating me so unkind?
I search everywhere but all I end up with is a love that never lasts.
My heart is a heart of pain.
It has never been able to love someone longer than it wants to.
I always love but does that person love me?
The answers to my questions are always painful.
Am I supposed to search the rest of my lonely life?
Where will I go and where will I search?
I'm tired of searching day by day.
Why must my heart be all pain and no love?

Heartbreak

Hopes, wishes, passions, and tenderness...
They were so close that I couldn't believe what was coming in my life.
All those hopes I had for us when the day was bright and the night was young.
When the day came the sun shined down and you were there to hold me.
When the night came you were right there beside me as we sat and watched the stars.
We had all of those wishes of not separating when tomorrow came, and we also wished for the distance between us to never be far.
There was the passion when you were in my arms.
You were my heart and you were the blood that went through my body.
There was only tenderness when you kissed my lips and whispered your lovely praises.
Everything in my life was about our love, but now they're only heartbreak.
I was broken hearted watching you go.
There was nothign but heartbreak watch the sun disappeared into the night while the stars hid behind the clouds.
I saw the heartbreak when I let you slip away from my hands knowing you'd never come back in the morning sun.

Heartbreakingly

Heartbreakingly, I've fallen in love with someone who doesn't love me.
I don't expect much from this person, but instead all I need is for her to talk to me and pretend she loves me a little.
I want her to touch my hands and look into my eyes like she really loves me.
When I first saw her I fell in love right away.
I didn't mind how old she was because I just cared about her.
Today, I don't care what people say, don't care what life has ahead for me, or what time holds for her and I.
I only want to be with her and only want her to love me.
Is it really hard for her to tell me a few sweet words?
Is it really hard for her to hold me?
Heartbreakingly, I've fallen in love with someone who doesn't love me.
She doesn't call or talk tenderly to me.
Still, why do I love her so much?
Why do I miss her when I know she doesn't love me?

Heaven Is Lost

One minute, the world stopped when you came into my life like a flower blossoming.
The next minute, the world turned and never stopped like the pain I was going through when you said goodbye.
You broke my heart and left me to watch as people walk on me.
Days and nights I was hoping one of these strangers was you.
Had there been another chance to look into your eyes and kept what I saw inside your heart, I would've never thought about the future.
All the moments that could be held, I held on tight and kept them in my heart.
Even if one day I'd die alone, at least I know I've held on to our love.
Yet, no matter what I do, I just can't let go of the fact that you're gone.
Heaven is lost at this very moment while I sit thinking about our dreams and memories.
Each minute is each kiss you left for me.
Each word is each touch you left on my body.
The dreams are still alive but the days have passed away.
With all the dreams we've had you went away.
Heaven is lost right at this very moment with the dying days and the fading dreams and love.

Hello, Goodbye

Yesterday, I saw you standing at the end of the road.
I wanted to walk over and say hello but after I took the the first step I changed my mind.
I didn't know what you'd say once you saw me.
I had so much to tell you but when I looked at you, the smile faded from my face.
Maybe it was the pain you left when you said goodbye.
What was there to say?
I asked myself what I would say to you if I were to walk over and said hello.
You probably didn't want to see or talk to me because your love for me was all yesterday.
Yesterday was a long time ago, and it could be the reason why you left in the first place.
Your heart had parted ways with mine, and you could never be the one who loves me like you once did many years together.
It only got worse when I stood there and saw you kissed someone else.
I wanted to let go of all the years and killed the memories of those happy days gone by.
I wanted to cry for the very last time to say goodbye to yesterday and to you, but I just turned and walked away.
I walked away from the pain like you walked away from me that very day.

Hold Me One Last Time

What kind of happiness last forever?
Like all the love songs, there's a beginning and an ending.
I thought it was going to last longer for us, and that our love would survive the end of time.
When we were in love I didn't ask for too much because you were already special.
You were all I dreamed of in those sleepless nights, and seeing you in my dreams made it all well by the morning light.
I told myself not to love you too much because once that day came, when your love ran cold, you won't see me the same way anymore.
I told myself not to put too much hopes in you because once it ended, it won't be too good for me.
And so that day came when you said goodbye and left me at the end of the road.
I told myself it was over and just let go because you' weren't coming back. Just let go because in your heart, my love no longer existed.
Yet, the love lingered on and there were times when I wished you could come back and hold me one last time.
Hold me with love, and let me have those feelings I once had with you yesterday.
I wanted to feel your love and wanted to be love by you.
But I also knew if you were to come back, it'd probably end the same way like last time.
In the end, I'd still be alone.

Time ~ Loneliness Of The Passing Hours

How Could I Have Known?

Can you give those days back to me?
Give me the sunlight and moonlight that shined on our love.
Give them to me like you did the first moment we met.
On the bench when we sat and talked, and when we first kissed.
Can you give them all back to me?
Can you see the sunlight is fading in my life?
Can you not see the happy expression that used to be on my face now is gone?
It's all gone because of you.
Can you give everything back to me like the day you brought happiness into my life?
How could I've known you were the sunlight in my life that kept me from dying?
I cherished and loved you, and when you left everything was black.
Life was blank and everything went dead like the silent night when I sat alone in my empty room thinking back on those gloriously loving days.
Can you give them back to me?
Can you give them to my heart?
Give them back all at once, all in one piece, to love and hold me again.

I Accept

I accept that my love for you was all a dream.
I accept that the first time when we met I was in love with you, and I'll always have to accept the fact that you're the only one I've loved.
You're the one I'll never be able to forget no matter what happens in the future.
Whether time dies or the world was to end, you'll always be the one I love.
I accept the passing days without you.
I know no matter what we say about love, and no matter how hard we try to go back to those golden days, there's no way we could bring them back.
Those silent nights lying next to you brought so much warmth and love.
I wish I could lie between you all day and forget about the world outside.
But no matter what I do, I'll never be able to have them again.
No words can block away the sorrowful tears and heartbreak I'm going through.
No tears can wash away the image of us.
No wind can blow away the memories you've left behind.
I accept all these.
I accept the truth that love hurts badly when you've finally found someone you truly love.

I Didn't Mean It At All

You know what I'm thinking about and how I'm feeling when I'm without you.
I say and do things before you that sometimes make you angry at me.
But always remember that I love you and never mean to upset you in any way.
I never want to bring tears or heartbreak into our love.
You know more than anyone else how much you mean to me.
How many times will it take for me to tell you I love you?
You should already know that I need you more than anything right now.
Through all the times together you should know me well.
My heart can't stand it when you're mad at me.
You should know I didn't mean it at all when I said there was no more love between us.
I didn't mean it when I said with or without you life would remain the same.
With you I laugh more and cry the tears of laughter.
Without you, I just die with the sad lonely world.

I Don't Want To Fade Away

I don't know how I can tell you that I love you with every minute of my life.
Yet, if I don't tell you now then I might never get that chance if one day you were to find someone new.
I don't want to fade away from your memory because you're the only one I truly love.
I could never love anybody else but you.
You shine and brighten up my life.
You're the sunlight in my life because when I'm with you everything in my life lives in harmony.
Without you I can't live a moment without thinking about the loneliness that surrounds me.
I can't face the light without seeing your smiles.
You care for me and I need that care every day and every night.
I need you like I need the air and water.
Don't walk away even if I don't tell you I love you.
I don't want to fade away because I don't want to be alone in love and in life.

I Have Lost You

I thought everything was perfect because we were happy and life was all well together.
All the memories we had were the greatest, and those memories were so dear and special to me.
This is why it's so hard to accept the reality of today knowing I've lost you.
You were my friend and only love.
I can't and will never forget you.
I can only live happy with you and only you.
Without you my life has broken up into tiny pieces, and there's nothing left to smile, cry, or love.
Sometimes, I forget that you're no longer here because I sit and wait but no one ever comes when Valentine arrives.
Sometimes, when I wake up, I forget that you're not here anymore.
I don't want to admit the truth because it hurts and makes me sad.
I guess everything that's perfect is always the worst of everything when that perfect thing disappears.
I have lost you even though I tried so hard to make you happy.

I Have No One Left

The day you left you took away my heart with you.
In the warmth of the night I waited but all I saw were the darkness of the night creeping up on my shoulders.
You made me stand in the darkness of the night waiting, and I had no choice but to wait by the minutes and by the hours.
When a heart has learned to love, it'll forever love the one who it has fallen in love with.
When a heart has learned what love truly is, it'll forever be in love.
Lonely, I waited for you every second with this heart.
Lonely, you walked away while I stood in the distance.
I'm still here waiting without knowing anything about our love.
I don't know how it'll be or what'll become of our love.
I don't even know what'll become of my heart as I continue waiting for your return.
Will I ever see you again in this place even if I wait for you forever?
I have no one left after you said you no longer loved me, and then you took off and left me with the night.
I have no one left but your image in my head.
In the night when I think about you, all I see is laughter and love between us.
So what happened to make you walk away?
I might never know because you'll never tell me.

Time ~ Loneliness Of The Passing Hours

I Said I Love You

I sit here on the edge of the river thinking about our love.
How time has passed by and swept our love away.
It seems like only yesterday when we met and you looked so innocent.
It seems like it was only hours ago when we spent our first night together, when you first held my hands, and when we first looked at each other and love grew instantly.
Maybe we had fallen in love too quickly.
Maybe you had wanted more than I could've offered you.
When you took my hands and I said that I loved you, did you feel the words that I was telling you?
Did you feel your heart move with my words or did you just take them in and let them out like you always did with others?
Now I sit here and listen to the water moving back and forth.
If only our love could be like the water, no matter where we go, we'd always end up where we had started.
No matter which direction the wind comes from, we'd never part.
I can't let our memories go like what you've done because what we had together are more than just lost memories.
I want to be able to look you in your eyes and once again tell you I love you, but I know I'll get that chance.
Whatever I say would only be for me because even if you're here you wouldn't care.
I want to look you in the eyes and ask you why you've left.
I want to look into your eyes and feel the love that was once there, but whenever I look I can only see my eyes looking back at me through the water.

I Wanted To Be Love

Our love was on the water and we were the leaves that kept on moving
without knowing where to go or what to do as the leaves faded away.
I wanted to be love by you and only you, but the love you gave me wasn't the
love I wanted to keep.
Your love was there only when you were sad and lonely.
I wasn't the one you truly loved.
You loved me because you couldn't find anyone to fill your lonely days.
Our love was like a boat lying in the middle off the water not knowing where
it'll sail to or which bay it'll stop at.
We had no place to stay and had no love for one another.
It was just pain and heartbreak.
How much heartbreak could I handle?
How much tears could I have given you when you came slowly then broke
my heart quickly?
You didn't love me and you never did try.
I wanted to be love by you and only you but you never bothered to look at me
and say you truly loved me.

If Only

How many hours and days will it take for you to turn around and love me?
How many years will it take for you to look into my eyes and tell me how much you feel for me?
I know our love is not a mistake and it's not a game.
If only you'd look into my eyes and tell me the truth inside your heart.
If only time could stop and let you tell me what's on your mind.
Would it be possible to hold you without you running away?
Why can't we touch when we're so close together?
Do we have to always be like this?
If only we could change what's right here, right now.
I want to hear your voice and see you without having to worry about today and tomorrow.
Is it that hard for you to hold me just once and really love me?
I hold you tight but you push me away.
I don't know what's wrong with me or maybe it's just you.
I don't know what you're thinking and don't really need to know.
Just hide from me and don't talk to me.
You've hurt me enough.
You've thrown my heart and love away.
If only you understand.
If only I understand.
If only we could see what's going on around us.
If only...

If There Was Another Chance

There was only one true love, and it was you.
There was no one else but you.
It was so hard to tell you I loved you.
Now, everything's over between us and I'm all alone.
If there was another chance I'd tell you I love you.
But the chance for that has passed by and there's nothing I could do to fix my mistake.
I've waited too long to tell you, and wasted too much time looking at you.
At the moment, I want to tell you something I've kept in my heart for a very long time.
If there was another chance I wish my voice would have enough courage.
Just three words but it's so hard to say.
I'm wishing and praying for another chance.
Another chance will come and I know I can make it through this last time.
Too many wasted time has passed and now I'm ready to tell you what's in my heart.
Tell you once and for all so I don't have to go crazy when I see you.
Tell you straight out so I can sleep peacefully.
I won't shake or be nervous this time.
I'll stand strong to tell you I love you, and forever, I'll love you.
If there was another chance then I would ask you to stay with me and never leave.

If You Knew

Why must it be so hard to find love but so easy to lose love?
If only you knew what you've done to my lonely heart.
Lonely heart, why do you beat so fast when you don't need to?
Why do you die when you don't have to?
I try so hard to find love but love never comes to me.
I can't cry or laugh, so what should I do when I can't find love?
No more tears, just a shadow on the ground.
I dream about love and daydream about the future.
Yet, no matter what I do I just can't find love.
Love comes happily and goes sadly.
I want someone to love but no one ever comes.
Don't ask me why and please don't tell me why.
I want to love but if I can't, I won't ask at all.
Love, if only you could hear me.
I want you to come to me.
I want to love and want to be loved.
I want happiness.
If only you knew what you've done to me my lonely heart.

If You Want To Say I Love You

We've been together forever but I've never heard from you the words that every lover wants to hear.
How many times have we walked this road when you've told me how you feel inside?
I want to hear the three words and want to hear you say them like you really mean it.
If you want to say 'I love you' then say it.
Don't contain yourself or hide those words when you know I want to hear them coming from you.
I need to know what you're feeling for me deep inside your heart.
Whisper these words, tell them to me, scream them, do anything you want and desire, just tell me.
I love you, and I know deep down, you love me too.
But now there's no time to be weak or shy when I really need to hear you say the phrase, 'I love you'.
Say it to me with love and care.
Our love is still standing in one place and not moving anywhere because I want you to say that phrase to my face.
Say it to my heart, and tell me you love me tonight.

In Love

Do you remember the moment when we were first in love?
Do you remember the moment when we first kissed?
Have they really died in your heart or is it just me who feels that your love is no longer the same like those beautiful dreamy nights spent together?
When you kiss me, I can't seem to find that special feeling like I used to.
Whenever you hold and kiss me, all of those feelings have died.
Whenever I look into your eyes, those sweet sensations don't seem to appear like they used to.
Maybe it's just me thinking wrongly about you.
Maybe love's just playing tricks on me.
It's making me think differently, or maybe it's really true that your love for me has faded away like all the kisses you once gave me.
Falling in love with you and being happy with you, they could never die.
I could never let them go even if your love no longer remains the same like it used to.

In The Distance

I hope this moment last forever.
I hope the sun won't come up over the horizon so we could be here forever.
If the sun rises and I forever walk away, what'll tomorrow holds for us?
What'll tomorrow be like without you?
What'll tomorrow be for you without me?
I hope we'll forever remember this moment together.
Tomorrow when we open our eyes, if the distance between us is only farther away, I hope we can cherish this moment tonight.
I hope you'll remember of me when you look up into the sky.
I hope you'll hear this special song playing in your ears.
Listen to the world go by and listen to the sounds of laughter.
Listen to the voice you've once loved and listen to the birds sing in the distance and remember of yesterday.
If one day we can be together again, I hope we'll remember that we had once fallen in love.
If one day, by chance, the distance between us narrows down, I hope you'll be the one standing next to me.
I hope you'll once again be the voice I hear and hope our love will last forever like we had always wanted from the very first time.

Time ~ Loneliness Of The Passing Hours

In The Nights

In the darkness of the lonely nights I can hear the footsteps fading away.
It is you coming or is it me thinking about someone who'll never come back?
Is it me or is it my heart not willing to let go of the night?
The night's slowly leaving me like the memories you've left behind.
Tomorrow, when the sun comes up over the horizon, I walk alone as the clouds slowly fade away into the sunset.
I'll still be here without you.
I'll watch the night comes by and think about you.
I'll once again walk down this road with so many memories.
On the fading footsteps, I'll think about you.
All the happiness will once again come back like a heavy burden on my gentle shoulders.
When the happiness fades away, I'll once again live with reality.
It's the bitter reality that you'll never come back like you always did.

July 4th

I walk this street like I have so many times before.
It's quiet as ever before, and there's nobody here but me and the night.
I don't hear footsteps or voices anywhere, but I do hear your voice whispering to me somewhere through my own imagination.
July 4th is here but where's the fireworks in me?
Like every other years I'm here in this empty space with no one to hold or share my feelings with.
Last year, I hoped I'd find someone to love and think about, but hopes and wishes have never done me any good.
I can wish and hope all I want, yet, there'll be nothing coming for me.
I long for someone to kiss these lips that have never tasted the feeling of sweet love.
I want to be held tight and want to feel the sensation of being loved by someone special, but when will I get these feelings?
Years have passed by and tears have gone dry.
I'm growing old and desolate, but does anyone know?
Does anyone even care?
This July 4th, I wish and hope like every other years.
I wish that this loneliness will melt by the next July 4th since there's nothing else to do but wish.
July 4th hasn't been so sweet and romantic ever since you left, and that day, the fireworks faded away from me forever.

Just One Wish

Many nights I'd stayed up late waiting for the shooting star to fly by across the dark sky.
Many nights I'd waited for the shooting star to pass by but the waiting was no use.
You'd left before I could make my wish.
You waved goodbye before the night was over, and you were out of the door before I could ask you to stay.
How cold I was here without you, and how lonely this bed was without your love.
Nights after nights there were so many shining stars.
They reminded me of you, how we'd sat together, and how we'd counted the millions of stars.
Each star represents how big our love was and how much we'd shared together.
It was how I meant the world to you.
Now I sit and count the stars alone.
I don't know how many there are up there.
Without you, there seems to be no more shining stars.
I have only one wish for us to be together forever but my wish was just too much for you.

Just To Know You're There

Yesterday, we walked on the same road.
Yesterday, you told me how the future would be for us if we were to stay together.
You told me you loved me and said you could and would never love anyone again as long as I was with you.
You told me as long as I loved you and never let go, you'd be with be until the end of time.
Yesterday, I was in love with your caring eyes and warm lips.
The lips that kissed me and the eyes that looked deep into mine.
I could never tell you a lie and could never let you go.
But it was all you in the end because you did let go.
When you left there was nothing for me.
You took away my love, heart, and every dream when we were still hand in hand.
Just to know you're there when the night comes and to know you're there when I feel lonely, it'll make me happy.
Yet, I know you'll never be here.
You're never coming back so we could live the happy days again.
The love has gone and there's nothing here but the dry leaves and flowers like our dead hearts.
No tears for you and no love for me.
We both have walked too far from each other.
We can never go back to those happy days.
Those happy days have died when you left with the night.

Just To Love And Die

I told myself not to love you too much.
I told myself to let go while I was not too deeply in love with you, but it was too late.
I was in too deep because the relationship between us was too far in.
We shared and loved too much that I knew one day when you walk away it'd be the worst day of my life.
I found out I was right when I stood there at the door and watched you go.
I had no one to turn or cry to.
There was no one to share my lonely days and sorrowfully nights with.
You left me there standing in the cold.
I stood there without knowing what to do or say.
Time was dying on me and my heart was dying with the times and days living without you.
I stood still listening to the crickets outside my windows whispering words to me.
I thought I'd still be happy without you but I was wrong.
I acted happy but inside I was dying.
Just to love and die slowly in your arms, so painfully and desperately.
I rather die fast and easy in your arms than to die slowly and cry forever.

Just You In My Heart

To have loved you and have you in my heart only once, and the rest of my life I'll think about you.
I'll cry as you lie to me and walk away as the tears slowly fall down on my cheeks.
To love you once is to die slowly without you.
I've loved you once and now I could never let you go.
I could never forget you and would never let you die from my heart.
It's just you in my heart and no one else at all.
Only you I think about.
You're the only person who made me laughed, but now, it's also you who've made me cry.
To touch you once is to cry an ocean of tears.
To kiss you once is to sleep with emptiness when you left without a single word goodbye.
To love you is to wait for you, your love, and your warmth to come back.
Just you in my heart, the one I love and the one who killed my life.
You're the one who broke the promises of love and joy of a happy life together.
Now our love goes up in smoke.
It burns on and on, and never to clear out again.

Kindness Within You

I'd love to see you again to have you in my arms and love you all my life.
I know the kindness within you and know there's no pain in loving you.
The kindness you had for me made my life so much easier.
You gave me a reason to live and changed the way I thought about falling in love.
At this moment, I want to hold you forever and never let go.
You always manage to take away the pain and tears in my life.
Right now, I want to tell you I've loved you forever and will never let go.
All I need is for you to tell me you'll be in my life.
I dream of you each night as well as each of the moments you're with me.
The kindness that's in you makes me feel so loved and appreciated like never before in my life.
I've never loved anyone like you, and no one has loved me like you do.
You should stay with me forever because no one will be like me, and no one will love you like me.
I've said that I'll always love you and I'll never change my mind.
We'll love each other until the end of time.
Just stay with me and don't go.

Kiss Me Before You Say Goodbye

I remember how I used to feel when you came over to my place.
The knocking on the front door excited my heart.
The feelings of that very moment when I had you in my life was great and special.
It was a feeling I couldn't explain to myself no matter how hard I tried.
But then one day you stopped coming, and I remember the last time I saw your face.
It was also the last time I held you and told you my deepest thoughts.
With all the pain in my broken heart I let you know how much love I had for you.
I told you all the fears I had about losing you but it didn't matter at all because even with all the words I spoke you turned away from me.
The last time I held you was also the last of the kiss you'd given me.
It was the last night I'd see you stepping into the house.
Today, I sit and look at the emptiness you've left beside.
I dream you'd come back and kiss me one more time to say goodbye.
The final kiss on my lips will make my life a lot happier.
A final goodbye and everything in my life will die away with you.
My pain and heartbreak will disappear when you give me the last kiss, and I'll be able to finally forget you in my mind.
I want to turn away from the door and not wait for that knocking, but whenever I hear a sound I think you're coming back to kiss me one last time.

Kisses On My Lips

Why is it so hard to find love?
Why is it so hard to find someone who truly loves you?
Someone who gives joy to your life without worrying about tomorrow.
Someone who loves you enough to make you forget about time and the world.
Someone who leaves kisses on your lips without the pain of tomorrow.
I always find love but love never exists, and love never finds me.
No one seems to be the right person who truly touches me with love and care.
Someone who never asks too many questions or turns away when I'm alone.
Is there true love in this world?
Will I find the person I'm searching for?
I'm tired of searching down the lonely roads that give me no promises for a better tomorrow.
Tomorrow seems cold when the kisses on these lonely lips are so far away.
So hard to see tomorrow and to know who loves you because you can't read someone's heart.
The road is wide and the journey is long, but it's never to be seen.
Tomorrow is so far from my heart.

Knowing To Love Is To Die

Knowing that to love you would only hurt me, yet to not have you next me, it'd hurt even more.
I rather love than not have you around because you kills away the loneliness that fills my life.
The pain you bring in our love is worth more than the loneliness in my life.
I rather love you and get hurt than not love at all.
You've come and gone in my life, and you've loved me once and hurt me so many times.
Sometimes I feel crazy.
I ask myself why I love you so much even though every time you're beside me you always seem to only want to hurt me.
I guess this is what love is all about in my life, only pain and no love at all.
Even if you tell me you hate me, seeing your face next to mine I'd die a happy person.
To have you with me in my life I'll be very happy.
I won't ask for more.
I only wish you could be beside me, and at the same time, you'd love and have me in your heart.
Knowing to love is to die, yet, I rather love you than have nothing to live for.

Last Day

This will be the last day I'll see you when I walk out the door.
Once the door closes behind me, I'll never see you again.
This will be the last day I'll hear you say goodbye.
I don't know when we'll see each other again.
This will be the last day I'll hold your hands and walk with you through this road.
Tomorrow, things will change and I won't be able to hear you say good-morning.
I won't be able to wake up next to you on the bed and never be able to hear the coming footsteps into my room.
Our love will change and we will change.
Last day to see you smile, but will I be happy or sad when I began to live without you tomorrow?
Should I be happy now that I get to see you before we depart?
Should I cry because our love has ended?
Cry because the seasons have changed.
Where should we be?
Where should we go?
There's nothing left but empty hearts and lonely roads because when we do walk these roads again I don't know if we'll recognize one another.

Late Love

I don't know what to say anymore.
My heart has stopped beating since the day you stopped coming to me.
My tears have started falling since the moments you stepped out of the door and never came back.
I don't have any more words.
I can't talk or sleep.
All I do is think about you.
I only hope that my love would never die in your heart and your love would never die in mine.
I wish we could go back to that heartbreaking day to fix all the mistakes and our love.
Yet, no matter what I hope for you'll never come back.
If only time would stop, if only I could go back, and if only we could relive those happy days again.
I'd never let you go.
I'd hold on to our love no matter how far you are and love you every second of my life.
I want to try and fix our love to relive those memories with you once again.
It's never too late in love to fix our problems and forget all those regrettable moments together.
I wish we could go back to the past and fix everything so that today would be a better beginning.

Laughing From The Heartbreak

Does anyone know my heart is broken?
No one really knows because of the laughter I show when I'm with them.
Nobody knows my heart is hurting because of one person.
Those days in love it was the laughter that made me happy.
Waking up in the morning next to the person I loved, it was everything I could've wished for.
But the laughter faded when the person said it was over.
Years have passed by but the memories still linger, and I don't think I could ever erase the person from my mind.
I could never throw away those wonderful memories.
My heart bleeds from the sad memories that were once happy.
I can laugh and laugh, and can lie to myself and my friends, but the tears from the laughter are the tears from the heartbreak.
Sometimes in the night I hear myself laughing.
The laughter echoes through the lonely dark room and I then realize that not all of the echoing sounds are laughter.
Some are the tears and sadness coming from my heart.
How can I erase anything when the person's love was so beautiful?
How can I erase that person from my memory when I still love that person so much?

Lonely Street

We used to walk this street in the silence of the night.
You held me tight in your arms with love and tender.
Where is that lovely moment today?
The lights now fade away as the night approaches but there's no sign of you.
Those happy times when we walked this street while you put head slowly down on my shoulder.
They were beautiful.
Today, like the daylight, those happy times have vanished into the darkness.
The kiss you gave me was the first and only kiss I'd remember for the rest of my life.
Today, my lips only taste the running tears falling down from my eyes.
Where have you and the love we shared gone to?
Those nights, how could we ever forget?
I live today with the lonely nights because I'm without you and the love I once had with you.
I miss you, and I miss the loving moments when you held me in your arms and kissed me goodnight.

Time ~ Loneliness Of The Passing Hours

Love Has Come And Gone

Those days together, whenever one of us made a mistake, all it took was a little kiss to make us forget and be happy again.
Those days together, every little lies meant nothing to us.
We loved each other and worked out all our troubles.
Today, it's just me trying to work out all the problems between us.
You no longer feel the same like I do, and no longer feel the need to make our love better.
Every time I look at you, you turn away.
Every time I try to work out our differences you never try to help but just walk off.
I don't know what has happened between us.
I don't know what's left for us to ponder on.
If love has really come and gone from our lives, I want at least to have one more day of happiness.
I need one more happy moment with you before the end arrives.
I want to hear you say you love me for the very last time.
I always try hard to get rid of our problems while you ignore them.
If love has come and gone in our lives then it's you who's given up on those happy days and all the happy time we had together.

Love Just Had To Die On me

I've fallen in love but this person doesn't know I love her.
She doesn't know I've been waiting for her these past few months to hear her say she loves me too.
I've wanted to tell her myself but I'm not strong enough.
She smiles and laughs, and everything else she does makes me fall in love with her even more.
I want to tell her but I don't want to lose her as a friend if she doesn't love me in return.
I've loved once, and like this love, I told her but she didn't love me.
She only wanted to be friend.
Time went by and we went our separate ways.
That love was sweet, and it was a love I'd never forget in my life.
I don't want to tell my new love because I don't want it to end the same way as before.
I wonder why love always dies in my heart when I love someone and never get that love back.
I don't want to be alone, but I rather be alone than to be heartbroken by someone I love but doesn't love me.
I can hide this love in my heart because all I need is to be next to her and it'd make me very happy.
I've learned from my first love experience that sometimes it feels better not saying anything than to actually say something.

Love Me, Love You

I can't tell you if it was yesterday or today that we met.
How time has passed by so fast.
I remember the first time you asked me if I loved you and then asked you the same question.
I hold that moment close to my heart and know you do too.
How many chances do we have in life to love?
How many chances do we have in falling in love?
I remember all our times together.
I remember what we had, what we shared, and what we loved.
I remember the first time we took each other hands and realized we'd be together forever.
Sometimes when I'm beside you I feel you're hiding something, but you never tell me what it is.
I know you love me, and you know how my heart only has you in it.
Sometimes our love is brighter than the sun, and then there are other times when our love is dimmer than the moonlight.
Regardless, I love you, and no matter what happens today or tomorrow, I hope we'll be together forever.
I'll always hold our love in my heart, and I know that love will bring us together.

Love You For Ten Thousand Years

When we were together I'd promised to cherish and love you for the rest of my life.
I made a promise I'd love you like no one had ever loved you before.
Today, though you've left, my promise of always loving you still remains.
Though you're no longer part of my dreams, a part of you will always remain in my soul.
I'll always love you.
I'd loved you then and will love you forever for as long as I'm alive.
I'll love you for ten thousand lonely years, and you'll always be the picture of tomorrow for me.
Even if I forget about the time and place in my life, I'll remember of you in my heart.
I promise you our love will live on for another ten thousand years, and I'll love you every second of my life.
When the seasons come I'll love you like the rain falling outside.
I'll dream about you like the stars shining above.
In the dark nights, I'll close my eyes and hope tomorrow comes so I can see your smile in the sunlight.
Even though you won't be there, I'll pretend the kiss in the wind is the kiss of reality when our lips lock together.

Love

What is love?
It sounds great and so pleasant when I hear of this word, but what is love?
Can you truly find love?
Does it always hurt when you're finally in love?
To love is to spend many lonely nights awake thinking, but thinking about what?
I guess I'll find the answer when I'm in love.
I fell in love once because I wanted to know what love was.
The love I found was nothing but a room filled with pain and sorrows.
Our love was a love of tears and mistakes.
We enjoyed our many nights but when those memories ceased, the person left me without saying goodbye.
Now, I want to say I know what love is but I really don't because I've never gotten true love.
I hope tomorrow I'll find love and get its true meaning because right now love is all pain and no smiles for me.

Loving You Hurts So Much

I didn't want to be without you but to love you was to hurt every single day.
To love you was to live a life of ache and pain.
You said to me you'd seen in our future and had plans for us.
You told me you'd be with me for the rest of your life no matter what happened.
I believed in your sweet words and all the lovely poetry you had written for me.
I thought the words on the papers belonged to me.
I took you in and let you on all my secrets, and I let you know things no one knew before.
You were the only one I trusted, and when you walked away I realized loving you would hurt me much more than just tears and heartbreak in those lonely nights.
I sat and wondered how long I would cry without you.
I wondered how long it'd take me to finally see the reality that you've left me.
I waited and waited for an answer from you but all I heard was the silence of the beautiful day.
Loving you hurt me so much from deep inside my heart and soul.

Loving You With All My Heart

Under the cloudless sky filled with stars we held each other in the warmth of the night.
In the silence of the night you took my hands and I held you tight.
You touched my heart, warmed my hands, and caressed me through the emptiness of those lonely days.
Yesterday, you held me close and told me you loved me.
Yesterday, you walked me through the nights and I wondered how long it'd all last.
Then, when you said goodbye, it was the answer to all my questions as all the tears of yesterday passed by without remembrance.
One day you told me you loved me and the next you changed your mind.
Under the cloudless night, I watched the stars shined and faded away slowly in the distance.
They seemed so close when you held me in your arms that I could've reached out and grabbed them.
When you walked away, the stars seemed so far away like the distance you had put upon us.

Lying To Myself

I told myself I didn't need you when you ended our love.
I told myself I could always find someone new who'd be better than you.
I could always find someone who'd love me more than you ever did; someone who'd take care and be with me forever.
I told myself many things but when the night came, I couldn't make it.
No matter what I did, I just couldn't keep my mind from thinking about you.
I couldn't stop myself from remembering of those tender nights when passion ran high.
Your face, eyes, and lips, I'd touched them once and now I couldn't forget.
Today, I lie to myself to forget the pain and anguish floating through my body.
I'll remember you for the rest of my life.
There's this emptiness in my heart, and there's a loneliness of love even though I've found someone new who loves me more than you could ever did.
But why is there this eagerness in my body to want to see and be with you again?
Why do I pretend I can live without you but when the lights go out I just wish that you were near me?
I'm lying to myself, I know it, but I can't resist the thoughts of you.
I can't find the feelings I had when you were next to me.
I lie to myself to hide the pain but I know I can never make it without you here.

Midnight Without Love

I can hear the clock ticking as midnight approaches.
I hear the silence outside the streets that are always crowded.
It has never been so quiet like this before.
I guess I'm not the only one alone tonight.
I'm waiting here under the glaring moonlight for someone to come into the door.
I've been waiting for a long time but the door doesn't seem to move.
I'm waiting for the moonlight to fade away with the morning hours.
I wait and wait, though there's no one coming.
There's only me and the emptiness of the night.
Midnight without love but I can't wait no longer.
Without love there's nothing left in my life but a straight line of nothingness.
I can't wait forever but what else can I do?
I can't cry or live anymore without you and your love.

Moments Of Mistakes

A few moments of mistakes and everything was gone.
One moment of misleading love and everything did go wrong as tears developed.
Love died, tears burned, and heartbreak and directions collapsed.
We had our moments of love and moments of tears, and yet, we overcame them all.
I thought we could love each other like we did day by day even though we fought.
We got mad at each other, we cried, and went through so many things together.
I thought we could go on but I was wrong.
You decided to walk away.
You wanted to see me hurt and see me die slowly without you.
You knew I could never live without you because of all the love we had together.
Yet, you still walked away.
There was nothing I could do or say to stop you from leaving.
The tears were all that I could give to you as I sent you away to your new life and your sweet new love.

Moments of Truth

Yesterday, I saw you walking alone and were heading toward my direction.
My heart beat faster because I was happy to see you again.
When we were up close, I smiled as you looked up at me but you didn't return a smile.
Our distance might have been close but your eyes told me we could never be the same again.
When you walked pass me without saying hello it broke my heart.
I turned to look as you slowly grew smaller and smaller.
The distance once again grew longer and farther away.
I didn't know what to do or say.
I stood there with all my heart and hoped that you'd once again reappear in the distance but there was nothing before my eyes.
It was like yesterday when the morning came and the hours grew longer without you.
I turned to walk away but my heart wanted one more desperate second to glance back hoping for a glimpse of your smile.
Somehow, I knew the smile that once belonged to me had gone forever.
I could never see that smile again because it'd forever passed me by.
I'd realized long ago you didn't love me anymore but the moments of truth always hurt when I thought about you.

My Loneliness With You

I never thought I'd fall in love nor find someone special in my life but here you are right beside me.
I've found you, the person who I truly love and want to spend the rest of my life with.
Every day, I wait for you to call.
Every day, I sit without listening or hearing as time flies by.
I walk to your place but you're not there.
I wait for you and your calls.
I wait and wait but I never get anything from you.
Your heart's empty and it doesn't have me or my love.
My loneliness is from you, and it comes when I'm not with you.
I don't want to think or hear about you but when I live without you I want you more and more.
You're my loneliness.
I can't live like this.
I can't think or see anything but you, and always just you.
I've never felt so empty like this until I met you.
Nevertheless, I've realized feeling lonely with you is better than not having you in my life.

Time ~ Loneliness Of The Passing Hours

My Love, If Only You Knew

Your love was heaven and it gave me more than the air I breathed.
You loved and treasured me more than anything in this world.
If only you knew our love was going nowhere from the beginning.
We acted like we really loved each other but we knew our love was never going to live on forever.
We were always reaching for each other even though the distance was slowing increasing.
You did give your best to me but it wasn't working at all.
When I had you, my life was heaven because it was warm and pretty like a spring day.
When I lost you my life was hell with a fire burning and the flame was annihilating all dreams and hopes.
I was your treasure and you loved me but you always saw me differently when something bad happened in our lives.
With such a relationship we had together, I didn't want to look back and smile.
If only you knew our love wasn't meant to be what we were hoping for.

My Love Is True

The morning sun, the happy times, and the moments of love are here with me.
This day is when our love blossoms with time and happiness.
The moment has come and the hours are passing by quickly.
The time we wait and the love we have now arrive to celebrate with us.
My love remains truthful to you and I'll always love you.
My love is true and I'll always give everything in my life for you.
Right at this moment you've left me even with the love I've given you.
Forever you walk your way and I'm here all alone in the moment of truth.
I sit here waiting for you but I know you probably won't come back.
My mind is lost because without you I can't think clearly.
The love we had, forever and ever, I'll remember.
The only question is, will you remember of our love too?

My Tears Are Burning Red

How could you leave me when I need you most?
You left without a word explaining why you no longer loved me.
You broke my heart and everything else in my life that came with your love.
How could you leave when my eyes were red with burning tears?
I cried and cried through the days and nights because I missed you.
When you were with me you were my only breath o flife.
Why couldn't you say the reason why you had to go?
You knew I was happy with you because you were my star and shining light.
I'd promised I'd never leave you and you'd promised you'd always love me but every word you said is now in history.
Our lives were perfect but you threw away everything.
We were perfect for each other but you wounded my heart and now I bleed slowly in pain.
My tears are burning red like fire.
I wish everything would be normal like the good old days together.
The days when my tears were of happiness and not like today when they are the red tears of heartbreak.

Nights Of Loneliness

Many nights I watched you sleep, and watched as you opened your eyes and smiled.
I sat and listened to you breathing in the placidity of the nights.
I wanted to be with you and near your heart.
I didn't want to close my eyes because every minute I slept was every minute I'd be without your love.
I thought by not sleeping and watching over you, it'd be all that I needed.
I thought you'd forever be lying here next to me.
I thought about many things and looked far ahead to our future.
I had many hopes, and thought for once, I could live forever in happiness but you weren't the one.
Now I sit here looking at the emptiness because you're no longer here.
I can't see the day or night without you, and can't live on with this emptiness in my life.
I want to close my eyes to sleep and dream about you like love has never died.
There're so many nights of loneliness as I sit and count the minutes and hours while thinking about you.
I think hard and try to understand why you're gone.
Nights of loneliness, from now on I'll have to face these many nights without you.
Nights of loneliness, where's the love that was here before?
Nights of loneliness as I count the days slowly passing by without you.

Time ~ Loneliness Of The Passing Hours

No One To Wait

I know it's kind of crazy falling in love with a complete stranger but whenever I'm with you I always feel the sun shining on me.
Whenever I see you smile I can't help but love you.
I know many people think we aren't meant for each other but in my heart I hope we'll be together forever.
I hope you'll always stay with me no matter what happens.
I hope one day when you decide to say goodbye that you'd tell me right away.
Please don't drag on forever because each day will only be more pain.
I don't want to wake up one day and find you gone.
I don't want to stand and wait for someone who'll never come back.
I don't want to wait forever for you only to find that you don't love me anymore.
I don't want to wait only to know you'll never come back to say you love me one last time.
I don't need false hopes in my heart if there's really no one to wait for in the end.

No Way Back

There's no way back to yesterday when hand in hand we walked down the road filled with love as I held you.
Lips to lips, I kissed you tenderly as you held me tight.
I still feel that moment in my heart.
There's no way back to the love we had now that you're far from me.
I don't know who you are anymore.
You don't love or have me in your heart like you once did.
I don't know you as much as I did once.
There's no way back to those roads we've walked before.
Those days seem like centuries away and could never come back.
We'll never be able to look at each other again like those loving days before.
No way back, there's no way at all to love again.
What have gone from us will forever be gone.
What we can remember and what we can forget, they must be the way they are.
No way back, no way at all.

Nothing Here But Tears

When I walk home I think about you every lonely moment.
Every step I make is every step in our love we've once walked.
Every word coming out of my mouth is every tear falling down my face.
When my steps fade and my legs stop walking, that'll be the end of all these remembrances.
I'll lose all of the love we've saved for the future.
There's nothing here but the tears of yesterday loneliness.
Those were the days of love when at night I walked this road and found my way home with you next to me.
Today, as I walk home in my own shadow, the footsteps have gotten tired and I've lost tracks of my way home.
Without you, I've grown tired of being lonely at night.
When will the footsteps be back?
When will you come back and walk me home?

Nothing Left But Memories

When we walked this road with you beside me I didn't think about tomorrow.
I didn't look any further but to be only with you, and I didn't know and care about tomorrow.
But now that tomorrow is here, perhaps, I should've cared more than I did.
When you walk with your new love on this same road, do you think about me?
Do you look back at those days and remember when we first kissed?
With your new love next to you, do you tell him what you once whispered in my ears?
Do you kiss him and leave a lasting memory with each other like we once did?
There's nothing left but memories like when you told me how we'd live together forever.
When you asked if I loved you, I thought it meant you truly loved and wanted to spend your life with me.
But all are gone and there's nothing left but memories.
Everything is gone now when I walk this road and remember of you, your face, your love, and your lies.

One Day In Love

I want to be close to you and tell you how much I love you but deep inside my heart there's something holding me back.
I can't seem to let those words out of my mouth.
Maybe it's because the first time I fell in love it was too much for me when love said goodbye.
Now, lying here together, I'm looking at you.
Eyes to eyes and lips to lips, I can already see I've fallen in love with you,
Yet, I can't tell you.
I don't want this love to end up like the last one, and don't want to hurt again in love.
Maybe one day when I'm ready for love and face the heartbreak, I'll let you know how much I love you.
For now, I have to look at you and dream about us.
I can't tell you what I'm thinking deep inside.

One Day Much Closer

The evening is slowly gone but why am I still waiting?
Maybe the love that's gone by is still wondering around here and making me think about you.
Maybe the person in my heart is still here somewhere waiting for me.
Perhaps, it's just me refusing to believe you've really left.
I miss those days spending the afternoon walking with you along the lake.
I miss those evenings walking with you down the quiet streets.
Those happy days are so close, but like the hours, they seem to have disappeared with the passing love.
One day much closer you'll come and tell me once again the lovely words in your heart.
You'll once again take me in your hands and we dance away the sorrows of the nights.
We'll kiss tenderly and wave goodbye to the loneliness you've left behind.
That day will come and we'll once again live happy under the blue sky.
You can smile with me and I smile with you.
We'll once again see those happy smiles that have vanished away.
We'll once again say 'I love you' like it really meant to be.
One day much closer you'll come back and I'll forget all about the sadness of today's emptiness.

One Day

One day, the sun will once again rise above the mountains.
One day, the happy smiles will come back and I'll forget that moment when your love faded away from my life.
One day, when happiness comes back, I'll stand and look you in the eyes.
I'll hide the pain you'd brought and hide the tears you'd given me.
I'll look deep within my heart and forget yesterday.
I'll forgive those moments inflicted into me with all the pain and sorrows.
I could never hate you for what you'd done because I was also the one who took you in my life.
I sacrificed my life and tears in loving you so I can't hate you for who you were.
I'll forgive those tender winter and warm spring nights.
I'll forget them, forgive the heartbreak, and forgive the lies that once I thought were truthful.
One day in the future I'll finally find your true love and keep it in my heart.

One Last Tear For Tomorrow

If you told me you loved me, then how could you walk away?
How could you take those words back like they never meant anything?
You took your words away like the wind pushing me aside.
You took my heart in your hands and I felt love and happiness, but then you crushed my heart and left me with the agony of love.
The tears of laughter we shared, did they mean anything to you?
The happiness we shared, did it mean anything or was it just another rainy day for you?
I gave you all that I could've given.
I swallowed the pain when you mistreated me and swallowed the tears when you played with my heart.
What more do you want?
Are you this cruel to just walk away?
Isn't there anymore love left in you?
Isn't there even one happy moment between us that makes you smile?
You walked away and couldn't even give me one last year for tomorrow.
Give me one tear so I could remember you by.
But you gave me nothing at all.

One Love Story

Once again, we sit here face to face and heart to heart without a word coming out of our mouths.
Once again, we look at each other in the silence of the day.
We smile at each other in the stillness of the night as we try to forget our love is no longer one love story.
Once again, we have to face reality and the heartbreak of saying goodbye.
This goodbye no longer means we'll see each other when the morning comes around.
This goodbye will be once and for all the waving hands of lost as you go your way and I go my way.
Eyes to eyes, there's no more love left in our hearts.
Things have changed throughout the days and nights we've been together.
Things have fallen apart and love has moved farther and farther away into the darkness of the night never to come back.
The smiles have drifted off and only false smiles and happiness remain here.
In our hearts, as we both know, the ending of our love story will end very soon before the night could say goodbye.

One Night Of Passion

You told me I was the stars, the sun, and the moon.
You wanted me to be with you forever and I believed those words.
I trusted you and gave my heart and life to you, but I didn't realize you only wanted one night of passion then it was all over.
I loved you whenever I saw you walk into my house.
Whenever the phone rang I hoped it was you.
I loved the way you talked and could listen to you forever.
I loved you and didn't want to let go, but you did want to go and I couldn't stop you from doing so.
One night of passion was all you wanted.
You never looked deep into my heart because you only wanted that one night of passion.
I didn't know how love was until I met you.
Why did you fool around with my love and then left me wondering?
I wanted to tell you so many things inside my heart, but I couldn't because I'd never see you again.

Time ~ Loneliness Of The Passing Hours

One Silent Night

One silent night you came back to me.
The face that had me dying in love during those happy days stood before me smiling with eyes still shining like the sun.
I closed my eyes and dreamed of yesterday but all I saw was darkness.
I opened my eyes and nothing was there.
No one was smiling.
It was just a gliding shadow of the curtains flickering in the dark empty room.
I closed my eyes to wish for those special moments when we were still in love to come slowly back, but there was nothing.
I could only hear your voice and the cold sad word of goodbye echoing through the darkness.
I heard the crying of the lonely soul.
For one moment, I thought it wasn't me and that it was someone else's pain.
One silent night I saw the moon smiling down on me and heard footsteps outside my front door.
I heard footsteps coming up the stairs but when I opened the door it wasn't you.
There wasn't anyone at all but just the wind blowing through the room.
It was just the cracking sounds of the doors but for a moment I thought they were our laughter through those happy days together.

Our Time Was Up

When you loved me, did you love me for who I was or did you love me for what I had?
Whatever I had, I gave them all to you.
I didn't know what more you could've wanted from me.
What I owned, I shared them with you.
I didn't know what more I could've given you beside my heart and love.
When you walked into my life, did you come with love or did you come with a plan?
Did you come to have fun, to love and hold me only to leave me?
When you walked into my life, did you want to share your love and heart with me, or did you just wanted to fool around with my heart?
How many lonely nights without you beside me?
You brightened up my life by giving me hopes and dreams.
Then there were those moments when our time was up and you didn't come anymore.
There were times when you didn't show up in my life and the next thing I knew you were nowhere to be seen.
You were so far and out of my reach and sight.
You were gone because you felt our time was up but there was no turning around.

Over The Heartbreak

There's always heartbreak in love when the first time you think you've really found someone.
You think this person would truly love and makes you happy only to find out later it isn't meant to be.
There's always heartbreak in love when you marry someone and think the vows you've taken really mean something until everything falls apart and everyone is crying.
There's always heartbreak no matter what anyone says.
No matter what you think or how you make love out to be, there'll always be heartbreak.
Heartbreak in the first moment and at the last very last.
Everything you do and say will one day turn out to be the heartbreak you think would never happen.
You go on believing you're over the heartbreak this person has left on you.
You'll once again find someone else.
You'll find a new kind of love that'll feel much better than the first.
A love you think will last forever this time around but then once again everything falls apart.
Everything in love, every word and lies, they'll all come back.
All the love will die and tears will melt.
Then one day you'll find out that love is nothing but heartbreak.

Pain You Give Me

Right now, I'm here in my room thinking about you and it's hurting deep into my heart.
Beside from you I can't think of anyone else.
I feel your presense like when we laid in this bed together.
Where have the hours gone?
It seems only yesterday you were here but now you're not.
It seems only a few hours ago when you asked me how I'd feel if one day you have to go and leave me.
I thought it was a joke and laughed, but now I'm crying.
You're never coming back, and when the sun rises tomorrow morning, I'll realize what you said yesterday was no joke.
You're not here and never will be again.
In the future, when we grow old, we'll never see each other.
The distance between us will get longer and longer, and we'll never be together like many days before.
When you get tired and sleepy, I won't be there.
When I get worried and sad, you won't be here to comfort me.
You're gone, you've walked out of my life, and forever, you'll never come back.
You're no longer a part of my life.

Passing Time

One day you came and told me how sorry you were about lying and hurting me.
You told me you didn't mean it when you left without saying goodbye.
You wanted to start over again.
I looked at you and stared at the face that was so warm and tender.
Within those eyes there were full of lies and painful memories.
The memories of love flashed by in an instance and I remembered how you'd left me that beautiful day.
It was a warm and sunny day.
The birds were singing, flowers were growing, and you were leaving.
I opened the door and you were gone.
You didn't care to write a goodbye letter.
I never saw or heard from you, and you never cared to call me.
Time had passed by and there was nothing left between us.
There was no more love in our lives.
When you came and knocked on my door, I didn't want to see your face.
Time had passed by and memories of you were all gone.
I closed the door on you like closing the memories we had shared together.
I said goodbye the last time to finally end the heartbreak I've felt all these years.

Pieces of Me

Is that the rain I'm hearing outside my windows?
Is it raining or are those my tears falling down outside?
Why should I cry knowing you won't come back?
Why cry when you don't care what'll happen to me when the day ends and I'm without you?
Even if the world stops turning you won't come back.
Yesterday is gone, and even if you're here, your love won't be the same.
Your love for me has died no matter what we do.
No matter what you or I say, our love is far away never to come back.
Pieces of me falling down on the ground like the leaves, and like when the telephone rings and I think it's you calling.
I could beg you to come back but what's gone is gone.
I can't change it and you can't change it either.
I love you in my heart, but in your heart, you don't feel the same for me.
You don't know and don't want to know that I love me.
The pieces of my broken heart are the happiness of your life.

Time ~ Loneliness Of The Passing Hours

Please Forget The Days Gone By

Is there any other night sadder than tonight?
I'm standing here in the middle of nowhere watching the night go by with no one to talk to or share my feelings with.
There's no one here to laugh with me.
Yesterday, you filled the emptiness in my life with your love and care.
Today, only loneliness and emptiness fill my life as the days continue passing me by and I can't look back to hold on to yesterday.
Above the star-filled night the moon slowly disappears like your heart and mind.
The stars fall apart like our love beneath the footstep of yesterday memories.
The love's fading away like the drop of rain when it touches the ground.
What to forget?
Who to get angry with?
No more hello or goodbye.
There's just me here thinking about love when love is no longer here.
Yesterday, today, or tomorrow, they're all the same.
Tomorrow, you'll come back and we'll love again, but only i tomorrow really exists.

Prayer For Our Love

Too young to love and too young to know what love really is.
Too young to understand what it feels like to love and be loved by someone special.
I thought I knew what I was doing but I was wrong.
I spread my wings and flew into your arms thinking you'd love and cherish me but it wasn't so.
I was wrong all along.
I was wrong in love and wrong in loving you.
The tears I cried were like rain falling down on the ground.
The tears I cried were like the prayers for our love to live forever.
I prayed to be beside you for eternity.
I hoped, wished, and desired every moment in my life would be spent with you but all you did was turn away from my love.
You broke me into pieces as you held my heart in your hands.
Too young and too much in love to realize you never loved me from the beginning.
Your eyes were looking at me but your heart was staring at countless others.
You never cared nor did you really loved me.
You never told me anything special when we kissed.
There were no special words, nothing at all.
You never wanted to be with me at all even though I desired otherwise.

Prisoner Of Your Love

I've looked for you through the darkest and happiest days of my life.
I've watched you through the pain in life.
I've longed for you, for your love, kiss, and warmth when you're around.
I can feel your love like the first time you looked at me.
I'm still in love with you like ever before, and is still searching for your love.
No matter what I do, I can't turn away from you.
No matter what I say, I can't let go.
I don't know what to do to let you out of this wounded heart.
I'm a prisoner of your love.
When you went away I spent all my time looking for you.
No matter where you went, I looked and no matter what you did I still loved you without regrets.
Prisoner of your love the day you came into my life.
I am and will always be a prisoner of your love.
I wanted you to love me and never let go.
I wanted you to loved me like when we first met.
But now I'm the only one who's feeling the heartbreak while you're somewhere happy with your new beginning.

Promises To Keep

A thousand words of love now are worth nothing.
A thousand words now combine into one broken heart that's beating in misery.
Nights and days of having to remember of you and each of the many promises you gave.
A thousand words are for nothing if none of these words meant anything.
When you took my hands and kissed me, they were memories I thought would last forever.
Nights of kissing and loving each other ended like the burning flame.
There were many promises but when you said goodbye they were only words gone by in the night.
You disappeared into the darkness while I searched for you in the night.
I cried for the caring arms through those nights and days living without you.
Nothing will change without you.
A promise you've given me, and then there were so many other promises.
Yet, they mean nothing now that I'm without you.

Quickly, The Days Will Pass

There aren't anymore words to say now that time has stopped in my life.
I have nowhere to go, and have no more worries or tears.
There's only an emptiness that surrounds my life.
We were happy together, and I thought we were meant for one another.
But the true was that you never wanted for us to stay together.
From the first very moment when you took my hands, your heart was cold.
You never truly loved me but instead only wanted to play with my heart.
You wanted to see me cry and felt my heart bleed.
The tears fell down like a river that led you away.
You were the boat flowing with my tears.
You never sailed back and I never stopped crying.
Now, I walk back and forth thinking and wondering if time will ever stop for you to come back here.
Quickly, the days will pass and our love will cease to exist.
Daylight will end and nighttime will come.
I won't sleep or eat but sit around thinking about you.
I'll think of the months we'd spent together and remember of the hours when the songs played and we danced together.
Quickly, the days will pass and I'll grow old.
Time will run out and I'll die without you in the days gone by

River Of Lost

This river has been the place where we'd spent our days walking and watching the sunset.
This is where we'd spent many passionate nights counting the stars and loving every minute of the time we'd held on to each other.
This is the place of love where you once came and knocked on my door.
In the tender and loving moment we listened to the sounds of the night in each other arms.
The slow moving waves of the river made our hearts beat ever faster.
Where has the time of love and memories gone to?
The lonely river of lost that was once full of love and joy now dissipates.
Time is still moving but our love has stopped.
It stopped moving with the passing days when you didn't look at me.
Love died in my hands when you walked away with the wind and forget all the love we shared.
You've forgotten all the dreams and promises we made.
You've forgotten when you kissed me on my lips and told me how much you cared for our love.
I know they are all lies today but it's too late.
You've gone so far away like the water that could never come back.

Time ~ Loneliness Of The Passing Hours

Road Of Love

Fate brought us together and gave us all of the world in our hands.
Our love grew that very special day on that road when you walked toward me and our eyes met.
We watched the sunlight filled our love and your smile took over my heart.
From that moment on I dreamed of you every moment of the night.
We walked the road of love and never turned back to wonder why we fell in love so fast.
Fate was in our hearts and love was in our heads.
Everything was pleasant and our lives were mystical.
But all that was yesterday and not the dark world I live in today.
Today, it's another story altogether as the sun shines down on this empty road.
This is our road of love but you're no longer that person.
This is now the road of tears and broken heart.
I don't want to think about you or what we did together yesterday.
Nonetheless, this road will always be a part of me.
This road is, and will always, a momery I can't change.
If one day when we cross path and you're with someone else, it'll hurt me badly.
But until that day, I'll keep your love in my heart and remember this road as the road of love.
I'll try to remember about yesterday and not think about the misery of today.

Road To Nowhere

Let us drink together.
Drink to the heartbreak of love and to the happiness that has come and gone.
Let us drink to forget the moments when happiness came, and to forget about that moment when sadness conquered our lives.
All the roads were laid out for me but I chose the road to your heart.
I chose you because I believed in your lies.
I believed everything you told me because I loved you.
Even today, I still believe you and still keep those words in my heart.
Reality hurts like a needle piercing through my heart but accepting your lies feels good.
The road to nowhere is what I'd chosen to walk on.
It'd led me to you and even through the tears and lies, I still love and cherish every moments we had together.
I don't want to show the pain I'm hiding in my heart because I know deep inside you don't care.
Through what I'd done and chosen in my life, all I wanted was your love in return.
Through the lies and passionate love, you were all I wanted.
Now, let's drink to everything to forget this moment and to live in a world without worries.
Let's drink to the lost love.
Let's drink to forget the road to nowhere which I'd taken.
Let's drink to forget all the lies and pain of love, even though a part of me still holds on to you.

Time ~ Loneliness Of The Passing Hours

Sad About Love

Love is a lonely journey that you don't know where it'll take you to.
Love is a lonely bay with many directions but no returns.
You fall in love and for what?
When the phrase 'I love you' comes out of your mouth, should I be happy or sad?
One day when you take back that phrase, will it hurt you more or me?
When love ends, what happens next for us?
I'll probably be sad about love, but is it sadness from losing you or loving you in the first place?
I know love can go from joy to tear, but I'm willing to take the pain.
Maybe it'll be the pain of losing love or just seeing you with someone else after.
I'll probably cry too, but crying is useless when I know if you could walk away once then you'd do it again.
Would I cry to have you back or cry to forget we once were together?

Sad Memories

One time falling in love and who doesn't know love causes a multitude of pain when the person says goodbye.
One time in love and who doesn't know there'll be more than just tears of happiness when love ends.
One time in love and why wouldn't it hurt when the tender moments die?
The days of walking home together during those beautiful summer days will disappear forever.
One time falling in love and when the laughter blacks out and fades away, the love songs end.
There'll be nothing left but a broken heart.
All beautiful memories fall down on the ground we walk on.
They'll die and whatever left will only be sad memories.
They are memories of the love when you sang those love songs to me during those winter nights.
No one wants to say goodbye.
No one wants love to end, but how long can love last when it always dies with the passing time?
Sad memories are for keep when words no longer come out of our mouths and when everything ends.

Sad

Sadness has taken over me knowing you'll be leaving soon.
I feel sad knowing our love means nothing to you even with everything we've shared together from the very first day.
There were so much love and tender moments together.
I'm sad to look back at yesterday and still hear you speaking softly to me.
Your words caressed me and your eyes looked deep into mine.
Those sweet words were the morning light, but today, they're the emptiness of the night.
Those words used to lift me up when I was down and carried me through the tough times.
They're no more.
Today, they kill me softly.
I don't want to remember what you've said yesterday.
Need to forget those sweet words and the hands that held me tight through the nights.
The hands that once held me in romance now no longer want to hold or touch me anymore.
I love you, but who'll love me?
I love you, but do you love me?

Shadow Of The Night

There's no one here but me and the night.
The silence of the night is walking with me along this lonely street we once walked.
I want so much to see your beautiful smile and hear you laugh like when we were in love.
The happiness in your smile was what kept me going day by day.
I want to hold your hands again and walk with you down this street.
I can still hear the music playing in my ears and hear you talking like you once did while we walked together.
Yesterday, the flowers were beautiful along this alley, but today, they're lying here dead like the memories you've given me.
In this lonely street I can still hear you laugh and see your smile.
I hear the footsteps pacing along in this street of memories.
I feel your love so close but when I turn to look there's no one but a shadow of memory.
A shadow of the night as I walk here all alone trying to remember of you.
I try to remember the happiness that was with me once and ask myself why our love has turned out like it did.

Sing To Yesterday Love

Looking at your eyes, there's nothing but emptiness.
What has happened between us?
Why has our love gone so dry?
Where have those happy days gone to?
One day you were laughing with me and the next I see your happiness going away from me.
I want to hold you close and feel your love but when I do all I feel is the separation and distance between us.
When you speak the warmth is not there.
It seems you have drifted farther away from me than ever.
I want to hold on to you but even if I have my arms around you, what would I be holding on to?
Would it be you and your body, or would it be your love and your heart?
Right now, I feel as though I'm a stranded boat in the middle of the ocean.
I feel myself drifting away from you like the water beneath me.
I can knell down and try to grab on to you, but you'll always escape from my hands.
If it were to be the other way around, I'd be the one waiting for you on the shore while you slowly drift away farther from me.

Smile To Hide The Pain

When you said goodbye my heart was dead but I didn't understand what I did wrong.
When you took my hands and gave me the ring I knew my life would never be the same again.
The last time you held my hands was also the last time I saw you.
When I was with my friends I'd laugh and smile to hide the pain.
They'd always ask me how I was feeling but I couldn't tell them the truth in my heart.
I couldn't let them see me crying and hurting.
When I was away from them I'd lie on the bed and think about you.
The silence in the room made me think of you even more.
The darkness and emptiness surrounding me inside the room made me missed you more than ever.
Nothing could fill me more than being with you right at that moment.
I smiled to hide my pain and to let people see the happiness outside, but my heart was crying out.
It was bleeding to let you know what I was feeling about you.
My soul was dying painfully just to let you know what I was seeing and hearing.
When the lights went out I was lying all alone in the room without your voice and warmth.

Sometimes

Sometimes, I want to tell you how much I feel about you but when we're together I just can't seem to talk.
Sometimes, when we're alone, I want to hold you close but then I just can't when I look into your eyes.
I want to hold you close and kiss your lips but something tells me not to.
Sometimes, when I'm with you, I smile but at the same time I feel scared.
I feel so very afraid that we would never walk this road again.
I'd cry without your love here.
Alone in the emptiness, I'd be too sad to wake up from my nightmare without love.

Stopping The Days From Passing By

I've learned to understand you through the years.
I've learned life with you could never be happy.
But since I've loved you, no matter what happens I'll be happy.
No matter if I'm happy or sad, you'll always be the one I turn to.
I've learned you can't ask for too much in life.
Being with you is what makes me happy even though sometimes you ignore me and would get mad at every little thing.
I can't stop from loving everything about you.
I hope we'll be together forever.
I'll stop the days from passing by just to be with you.
All my youth, love, and life, I'll give to you and all I ask in return is that you love me too.
No matter what you say or do as long as you love me I'll forgive and forget.
Just don't ignore or stop talking because that'll bring pain to me.
I want to love you forever and want you to do the same.
When you're sad or happy, share that happiness with me.
All the sad and happy times we'll share together and everything that you do I'll learn to love you for them.
I hope in return, you'll do the same.
Love me for what I am and love me for whatever that I do because I'll do the same in return.

Sweet Love

I can feel the wind changing and feel the happiness slowly dying in my life.
I don't know if you're seeing what's in my eyes.
I don't know if you still feel the same way you did when we first fell in love.
There're so many things I want to tell you but I don't know how to express my feelings.
There're so many words in my heart but I don't know if this is a good time to tell you.
On the other hand, if I don't tell you now I might not be able to tomorrow because I don't know if I'll see you when I wake up.
I don't know what you'll say when you look at me in the days to come.
I don't know where our love will lead us.
I just don't know anymore.
I'm tired and can no longer get those feelings of love when I'm close to you.
I no longer see the love you have when we lie down together or when you kiss me.
I feel our love drifting apart, and feel your love falling deeper and deeper away from my reach.
What more can I say and do to be happy with you?
What more can I wish for when there's nothing ahead?
The sweet love is gone and the sweet dreams have died.
We're slowly parting ways.

Sweet Words

First, you told me we'd be great friends.
For awhile, we were just that but then slowly your sweet words pulled me in and I fell in love right away.
I was so in love and forgot the time and day.
All I knew was to love you, and now today, I sit here with tears of laughter.
I laugh to forget you and cry because of your lies which I believed in.
Those sweet words, how lovely they were where you gave them to me.
Today, those sweet words are the arrows that pierce through my heart.
Your sweet words were tender like the music playing in my head.
They were the love songs you dedicated to me.
Those words were printed on the poems you said you wrote for me.
I felt crazy in love with you and gave you everything.
I trusted you too much and loved you with all the seconds in my life.
You gave me sweet words and I lived with them.
Now, I feel sorry for myself and feel stupid that I didn't see how you never truly loved me.
You'd written all those poems to lie and fool with my heart.
I see everything clearly now but it's too late.

Tears For You

The river we walked by when we held each other tight and love was the sunlight above our heads.
Everything was real between us without any lies.
The river of love when you told me how beautiful I looked.
Today, the river lies empty without you.
You were the one that kept it alive when you were still in love with me.
You kept it happy when you said you'd never leave me.
I believed the lies and thought you'd never go.
I thought you were the one who'd been sent from above to love and care for me.
But like the water, you came and slowly drifted away.
The tears I cry today are for you.
The love, lies, and happiness of walking on this river mean nothing today without you here.
I give these memories back to you.
I give you back the lies along with my tears.
I never wanted to love but you wanted me to.
When I finally loved you, you walked away.
Tears for you, like a river that flows and flows.
I'll cry for you and your lies.
I'll cry for your love, the love that came and went like the water.

Time ~ Loneliness Of The Passing Hours

Tears Of Love

The day our love died, nothing in my life was the same.
Everything broke piece by piece, and whatever we had together was gone.
Those days and nights together sat in memories, and they lingered like the pain in my sleep.
I wanted to hold you like holding back our memories.
I wanted to stop you from leaving because I knew once we were apart you'd forget all we'd shared.
Tears of love were different than tears of sadness, but in the end, it was all the same when you hurt deep inside.
Tears of love were hard to see but easy to make when you said goodbye.
The tears of love I cried represented each memory we had.
I wiped my tears like erasing our memories.
Love was full of tears and sadness but it was hard to find love.
My heart was easily broken when you killed our love.
Nothing was left here but darkness and sadness.

The Day Of Loneliness

If we could go back to the past I wish I could make things better between us.
The first time I saw you I thought we could never be together.
I never gave you all my love, but through all those times spent together, we fell in love.
When I found out you were the one, it was too late because you never loved me the same way.
Every word I gave, you thought they were lies.
Everything I told you, you never took seriously.
I couldn't blame you because I was the one who lied in the beginning of the relationship.
Telling you the truth later on was too late because you no longer loved me.
If we could go back to the past then I'd hold you tight and tell you I love you.
If we could erase those false happy memories and in return make real happiness, I'd give everything in my life for you.
If we could go back and take away that one day of loneliness then I'd hold you forever and never let go.
The day of loneliness when I told you I loved you and you only laughed at me.
You thought I was lying but in reality, I really meant what I said.

The First Time

The first time I saw you smile I was so in love.
The first time you touched my hands, I lost my heart and mind.
I was so in love I forgot the time and fell into your world.
I left everything behind because loving you was all that was on my mind.
I spent days and nights thinking about you.
I couldn't read, write, or did anything but think about you.
Your smile, kiss, and beautiful face were everywhere.
I turned to my left and saw your face.
I turned to my right and saw your smile.
I didn't sleep late at night wondering how lovely it was be when we were together.
I could feel you holding me and kissing my lips.
I was a fool in love and a fool to love you.
When I saw you with your new love, it broke my heart.
I couldn't cry because there were so many tears in my heart that I wanted to let out.
My heart went dead and I couldn't sleep as I wonder about you in the night.
The first time I saw you smile, I felt in love right away.
Then the first time I saw you with someone else, my heart died with the love I had for you inside.

The Hand Of Time

Watch the days go by and regret what you've done.
Watch the days go by and think about yesterday.
Think about the memories you've left behind.
Were the memories lovely and peaceful, or were they just memories that break your heart?
Watch the days go by and feel sad about what you've lost.
Feel sorry that you couldn't tell the ones you loved the last word goodbye.
Watch the time goes by and think what'll be tomorrow.
Think back about what was there before and what has changed now.
Is it the love you have for me that you can't remember?
The gentle love that you brought to my life but then took back.
The hand of time, if only I could turn back and kiss you one last time.
I won't tell you I love you and won't look into your eyes because then, when you walk away, I wouldn't have to face the fear.
When you walk away I wouldn't have to sit and think about the love we've had together.
The hand of time, if I could turn back yesterday, I'd never forget your love.
I'd hold on to it so when you walk away I wouldn't have to feel alone.

The Last One I Trust

From the very beginning, my heart was already in a fragile state.
I thought when I broke up with my last lover it'd be the last time I'd ever trust anyone.
I thought that person would be my last love forever.
When I found you, I resisted your love.
I tried not fall in love but you were beautiful and your words were smooth.
Your eyes looked deep into mine and I knew it was time to move on.
I let go of my old love and gave you a chance.
I tried and love all over again.
When I finally settle in with you, things were perfect.
Days and nights went by as we talked and drank through the sunlight and moonlight.
We felt into our own world of love where we were the only two.
I thought this was it, that you were the real love of my life.
But like all the others, it was a quick goodbye.
The last one I trust, you were the only hope left in my life to be happy.
I wanted to live those days of happiness but you took that away.
You were the last hope, but maybe it wasn't meant to be from the start.
My last hope was left on you but it was just another wish that flew away like all the other wishes that'd gone by years after years.

The World Doesn't Know

When I see my friends, I smile and talk normal to them.
I show them no signs that I'm heartbroken.
When they ask about you, I tell them we're very much in love.
I tell them we're so connected we couldn't bear the thoughts of not seeing each other every day.
I tell them many lies, and deep inside, they're tearing me apart.
When I wake up in the morning, I ask myself why you're not here.
I twist and turn in bed at night wondering why you're not beside me.
When I have one of those terrible nightmares, I open my eyes hoping you'd be here but you're never there.
Reality strikes like a bolt of lightning when I wake up to the truth that you're really gone.
The world doesn't know and nobody knows anything anymore.
The world doesn't know underneath this happiness there's so much pain.
There're so many lies I can't bear to tell.
I can't tell anyone or reveal the truth inside my soul.
The world doesn't know that with all the laughter in the morning and happiness at night that when the lights go out I'm all alone.
I'm with no one but myself.

Those Happy Days

The lights have gone out and the night has come.
It's just me walking this road alone.
Those memories of you and I flash by like the stars shining above the sky.
Those happy days together are buried in the silence of the night.
That moment when you knelled down and kissed me goodbye, that was the last kiss and happy day in my life.
With all despair and loss, you walked away with this heart waiting for you.
Silently, I waited as the days passed by without your sight.
The kiss you gave me now I keep forever.
You've chosen your own way and there's nothing left here for me.
I die alone as the night brings the silence without the love of those happy days.
Slowly and breathlessly, the night takes me away.
The sweet words you told me to keep, were they really mine?
Did they belong to me or did you use them with someone else already?
Those happy days sitting together and watching the nights went by.
I looked into your eyes as the sun went up over the horizon and shined brightly on your smile.
Those happy days have gone by like the silence of the night when I turn to look and find nothing but the loneliness of the morning light.

To You, With Love

To you, the one I've loved with all my heart.
My love for you is still the same like always.
Though you've left, nothing here has changed.
Your love, kisses, and warmth are all here with me.
Though the tears have washed away all the pain in my heart the day you wanted to go and find someone else, my love for you remains faithful.
Sometimes, I'd ask myself how you could've walked away and forget all the moments we've shared.
You've forgotten those nights and days together.
You could forget and walk away from me, but I'm different than you.
You were my first love and you'll always be.
Even if tomorrow I find someone else better than you, the pain of you will remain.
You were the first love in my life and will always be carried in my heart, my soul, and my mind.

Today Or Yesterday

Today or yesterday, which one would you choose when you and your love sit together drinking coffee or wine?
Which one do you prefer?
Do you prefer your new love or me better?
When you hold hands and walk down the road laughing together, do you remember yesterday?
Maybe you only pay attention to what's before you.
Do you love today better than yesterday?
Do you love what's in your hands and forget about me?
Your love was like the sun that shined down on my eyes.
When I met you I loved and needed you in my life.
You stayed with me for some good moments and gave me the love and support I needed.
When the nights faded, you went away.
Is today much better than yesterday?
Is your love more than what I was to you before?
Does your love have more than what I had to offer you?
There're so many questions and so many things I don't understand.
I'll probably never be able to understand since I'm without you today.
Today or yesterday, which one do you choose when the music plays and you dance away with your new love?
Is the music more tender now, or is it the same music you played for me when our love was still alive?

Tomorrow Is Unknown

Tomorrow, when I close my eyes and lie down to sleep forever, what will happen to us?
Will you come back like you did when I was young and beautiful?
Will you come back like when you loved me and told me I was all you had?
When the silence in my room fills the night and when no one is here but the shadows and laughter of yesterday, will you cry for me?
Will you cry the tears of lost and love?
The tears you never gave me even on the day when we broke apart, will you finally give them to me?
Tomorrow is unknown like your love.
When I had you, I thought your love was all I needed.
When you walked away, I realized you weren't love but instead the pain in my life.
Now, I close my eyes for the sleep of eternity.
Where are you?
Don't you care to come back to see me?
Do you care at all what's happening here?
Are you happy with your new love and life that you don't even remember your home?

Tonight, One Last Time

Tonight, for the last time, you'll spend with me and tomorrow when the sun rises you'll be gone.
Tonight, one last time, we'll sit and look at each other.
It won't be the same like we've always done so many times before.
Tonight, one last time, we'll hold each other in our hands and hearts.
Tomorrow, when the sun rises, your hands will be gone forever from mine.
Your eyes will no longer look deep into mine.
You'll no longer remember the touch and feelings you've had with me.
Tonight, one last time, let's be happy together.
Just be happy for me and let my heart smiles for the last time before the pain takes over.
When I wake up in the morning and you're not lying beside me, it'll be a new lonely day.
Tonight, one last time, let's put away the sorrows and be happy.
Laugh with the night so that when you're gone my heart will remember of the happiness and never remember the pain of losing you.

Under The Sand

On my way home yesterday I saw someone standing at the end of the street.
I stopped, frozen in my track, as I stared at the face of that person.
I walked up to her thinking it was the same person who'd left me.
When I saw the face up close, I realized I was only mistaking.
I felt sad realizing she wasn't the one I've been waiting for.
I want so much to be able to find you again, but no matter where I go, I can't seem to find the right direction.
All the love in my heart is dying without yours.
All the memories of yesterday dry up inside like the sand without the ocean.
The footsteps on the sand have now disappeared with the crashing waves like your heart crashing my love when you walked away.
Under the sand, the memories lie deep.
Under the sand, the words of love are still buried and very clear.
The love is still sweet but you're nowhere near.
You're gone and there're no directions that can take me there to you.
You're the waves that come in and out like all the pieces of my broken heart.

Valentine Day

I remember the first Valentine's Day with you.
We'd just met and our hearts were blossoming with the seasons.
The flowers you'd given me are still here and they're as beautiful as our love once was.
The red roses still smell the same, but I wish I could say the same thing about our love.
Last Valentine has gone by and I can see the flowers dying soon.
They'll fade away like you have since last year this time.
The love is still here, but where are you?
Who's taken you away from me?
Does that person love you more than I do?
Wherever you are now, do you still love and think about me?
Is your new love more special to you than our old memories?
I'm here waiting for you to come back and wish you could feel my heart aching for you.
Wherever you are, are you happier than you were before?
Are you truly in love or are you just waiting to break another heart like you did with mine?
Maybe your heart is like a bird that flies and flies and never stops in one place.
If to really love one person is to die softly, I'll sacrifice to love and have you back in my life.

Valentine's Loneliness

I wonder how long it'll be before I find my special Valentine.
Every year it's the same, with no love or someone to share the things in my heart.
All there is in my life every time this year is the Valentine's loneliness.
How many lonely hearts are out there when February comes?
How many lost smiles are there beside mine?
There are lots of questions but no answers.
I don't want to be alone when Valentine arrives.
I see lots of lovers walking down the streets fill with happiness and romance, and then I look at myself.
They feel more while I feel less, but maybe I shouldn't complain or be sad.
Maybe loneliness is the best for me at this moment.
Maybe every Valentine's loneliness is meant to be until the new beginning comes.
Every year is the same with this lonely heart of mine.
I hope my love will come to ease my Valentine's loneliness.

Waiting For Tomorrow

Those days that were with us were the days of love.
Though knowing the hands that held me close while walking home at night won't be here forever, I still hoped.
I could already see the dreams I had about us each night slipping away slowly within our reach.
The loneliness crept up knowing you weren't going to be with me forever.
The tears could no longer be kept inside knowing the months ahead won't be as happy when they come and I'd be without you.
I could see you no longer felt the same way about me when I touch you.
The warmth had disappeared and I could feel the pain in your heart.
I tried to understand whether the pain was from losing me or being with me.
You were no longer the same person I knew before.
You no longer laughed or smiled when we were together.
I was waiting for tomorrow to come so that our happiness would be here forever, but that wasn't so.
Once your heart changed, I no longer had you.
I waited for tomorrow and when it finally came, I had nothing because you were no longer the same person who kissed me.
You looked into my eyes but all I saw was emptiness in your heart.
I was waiting for tomorrow to come, and when it came, I lost everything I had with you.

Waving Goodbye

I feel afraid to love again after I let you go.
I'm too afraid to say what's in my heart to someone else after our love has gone so wrong.
Did you see the end before I did?
Did you feel something wasn't right in our relationship?
If you did, I wish you'd told me so I could change somehow to make you happy.
Why didn't you warn me before you decided to go?
I'm still here thinking about us and still haven't fully let go of you.
I didn't want to wave goodbye.
Our relationship was going well, but maybe that was just me thinking way too deep.
I said goodbye to love like waving goodbye to a beating heart.
My beating heart was waving goodbye to you even though I was giving you all my life and soul.
It's killing me now knowing what love really is.
Loving you is trying to let go, but somehow, I just can't.

What Should I Do?

When we held hands and walked down that road, I thought we had everything.
I thought our love would last until the end of time.
When we kissed and held each other more tenderly than ever, I thought we'd never fall apart.
Yet, today, all my thoughts have vanished away forever.
You left without a single regret on the memories of the good times we had.
Today, I want to cry whenever I think about you even though I try hard not to.
I can't see or hear anything beside your voice because it lingers around me.
What should I do now?
I hear my heart dying without your love.
You're now free from all sadness while I'm here holding on to you.
I'm waiting and wanting something that doesn't exist anymore.
I ask you, what should I do?
What should I do without you?

Time ~ Loneliness Of The Passing Hours

When I Learned That I Loved You

Each time you held me in your arms I just couldn't help but fell in love with you.
Each time you told me how beautiful I was I just couldn't stop but to look you in your eyes and fell deep into your heart.
You were affectionate when I was with you.
I wanted to tell you how much I loved you from the inside of my heart when you held me.
When I learned that I loved you my heart ached so much because I didn't know what to do.
I had many things I wanted to say but my heart told me I shouldn't.
So I kept my love for you hidden because I wasn't sure if you loved me at all.
I didn't know what you were thinking inside or what would happen if one day you'd walk away.
I was always afraid, and didn't want to ask or tell you about my love.
I was afraid of losing you even though I didn't know what you thought of our love.
I wasn't sure what our love and my life would be like tomorrow if you didn't love me.

When You Walked Away

When you walked away there was someone you'd left behind.
She was still in love with you and waited for your return.
She'd promised to love you forever and never would change.
The years have gone by but she's still waiting.
The love for you is the same and the promise remains.
The love that once belonged to her now is no more.
The eyes that once looked deep into hers now belong to someone else.
The first kiss is buried deep inside and the sensation still lingers on but the old flame is gone.
You've walked away leaving behind someone who loved you so much.
How could you've walked away without feeling guilty of what you'd done?
The warm nights spent together and the love shared, did they mean anything to you?
How could you have forgotten everything she'd given to you and walked away?

Time ~ Loneliness Of The Passing Hours

Where Have You Gone?

The sadness that I have I could never put into word.
The night is filled with lights in the quiet streets.
The midnight hour approaches and I'm up trying to savor whatever I have left with time.
There are people out there walking, and they're ignoring the night just like me.
Knowing that you're never coming back, yet I still wait.
The night is full of passion and the stars shine brilliantly, but you're not here to witness this moment with me.
Where have you gone to?
The moon is moving in the water like your face smiling back at me.
Every night, I walk the many streets or sit in my room and wait for you.
I watch the people go by and hope one of them is you.
Sometimes, I don't care about the world because all I want to do is sit and wait.
I'm waiting for someone who'll never come to the garden of love.
Every second and minute that pass by bring the night ever closer to its end just like our love.
Where have you gone?

Who Really Knows?

Could anyone run away from love when he's finally found the right one?
I've asked myself what I'd do when that day comes.
Just think how magnificent it'd be to fall in love and build a lifetime of memories with the person you love.
But then again, how will I handle the pain when this person no longer loves me?
What would I do then and how would I feel?
Will I smile to forget the hurt in my heart or cry because my love left me for someone else?
Who really knows what'll happen in love?
When love comes there can be lots of happiness, but the pain is always lurking around.
It's waiting for that moment to hit you down and make you feel as if the world is ending.
And then there are those tears that are always around you.
There are those tears of happiness in those many passionate kisses that warm your heart as you talk all night while sharing beautiful moments together.
Then there are those painful tears when your heart stops beating and you're crying through the loneliness of the night.
Who really knows what'll happen when love comes?
I'll just have to wait for that day to come.

Time ~ Loneliness Of The Passing Hours

Why Do I Love You?

Even through all the pain you've caused I still love you.
I think about that night when you walked me home and then slowly kissed me goodnight.
Little did I know it'd be the last time I'd see you.
The last word spoken by you would really be the last word.
I want to understand what had gone wrong through these falling tears.
The hurt runs deep, but still, why do I love you?
I don't know why being with you makes me so happy even though at times you don't care for me at all.
Whenever you call me on the phone, I just can't refuse your love.
Don't ask me why I love you so much because I can't say myself.
Why do I keep on falling in love with someone who breaks my heart so many times?
Maybe I can't tell the different between love and misery anymore.
When I'm with you I get both, so why can't I just forget about you?
Whenever I close my eyes I think about you.
I don't want to know why I still love you in my own craziness, but I just need you back.

Wishing Upon The Moon

I wish this moment would never end.
I wish the hours would stop forever because once they move on I'll never see you again.
We sit under this full moon romanticizing about what'll be tomorrow.
We look in each other eyes and wonder what tomorrow will be like when we say goodbye tonight.
I hold you tight at this very moment, but I can't hold you in my arms forever.
When morning comes we'll have to say our goodbye.
I don't want to let go, but what choice do I have?
Maybe tomorrow we'll be together again or maybe in another life we'll meet again.
We'll fall in love again, but by then, our memories of tonight will forever be lost.
No matter what happens, I hope our hearts will lead us back together.
When love once again blossoms in that unknown place tomorrow, we'll once again stand under this full moon wishing for a better ending.
A happier life will be for us under these shining stars.
For now, we can only sit under this full moon wishing for the night to never end.
Once the night comes to an end, we'll have to let go of everything we have and forever be lost in time.

Without Knowing

The games we played when we were young are still in my head.
Time has gone by so fast that things have all changed from those innocent days.
Do you still remember those times when I chased you around?
Do you still love those songs that used to play on the radio?
Most importantly, do you still remember me?
The quiet afternoons sitting under the sun still warm my heart like ever before.
If I'd known that things were going to turn out like today, I wouldn't have let you go.
It's too late to say I love you and that I'm sorry.
Without knowing how our love would be, what was I suppose to do?
I wish you were still here listening to me sing to you those songs.
Those carefree days sitting together watching the clouds roll by are no more.
I wish I could turn back time to have a better ending, but time doesn't go back.
Can you take back the wind when it has gone by?
Can you put back the water that has move on?

Words Of Love

Has there ever been a moment when you asked me to dance?
Has there ever been a time when you kiss me without me asking?
Why are you giving me all these words of love when you can't prove this love to me?
Is it because you're afraid to love?
You're always waiting for me to make the first move.
Maybe I'm just as crazy as you are to still love you.
Maybe it'd all be better if I just go away and forget about you.
But then again, maybe the reason I've been staying with you is because I really love you.
Without those words of love, somehow, I still need you in my life.
I want to run away from it all but too afraid to lose you.
If only you know that all I need is something deep in your soul.
Just prove a tiny bit that you truly love me.
Give me a few words of love I want to hear because that's all I need from you.
Don't let me wait forever because time isn't with us forever.

Wrong One To Love

The first time you meet my friends, they all told me you were the wrong one to love.
I ignored them because I loved you and thought in my heart you felt the same.
You treated me well and never hurt me in any way.
I believed in our love, but as time went by and things slowly changed, my friend's advice was right.
There were times when I took your hands and there was no connection between us.
I felt nothing from you and wished you'd told me what was going through your mind.
From the beginning, I thought my friends were wrong about you.
I thought my heart was on target choosing you, but sometimes your heart can be wrong.
I gave everything to you, but our love went from good to bad.
How did our love end that way?
I could say now you were the wrong one to love, but it's too late.
Was it me or you who killed our love?

You Always Lied To Me

We told each other we'd always be truthful and never lie to one another.
We promised that we'd always love and never to hurt each another.
You promised me we'd be together and I saw a bright future a head.
I gave you my love and trust, but in the end, I received nothing.
Through all the happiness, you were only lying to me.
You always lied when I asked you if you loved me and you said yes.
Maybe love meant something different to you than it did for me.
You never took our promises in your heart, but instead, you threw them away.
I lived through your lies and now the future is here and I'm to myself.
You lied to me when you told me I was the only person you'd ever loved.
I want to take back the kisses and passionate nights with you.
I want all my memories of you gone, but right at this moment ,they're all I have of one beautiful dream.

You Are Gone

If only you could be the moon and stars above the sky shining down on me when the night comes.
If only you could be the sun and blue sky that brighten up the day when I walk alone on the edge of the bay.
The bay is dry and dead because it's waiting for you like waiting for the rain.
Nowhere in this bay lies your love or the secrets you whispered in my ears.
Nowhere are the kisses you gave to me in those days of love and freedom.
My lips are dry like the bay itself waiting for your lips.
I'm waiting for you to come and take away this loneliness.
Come and break down this prison of sorrows.
Give me your love and take me away into the night to forget that you're really gone.
Fly me away from this prison of love whenever I'm without you.
You're gone and I don't know where you are.
What have you done to our love?
What has your love done to me?
The days are dry and the bay is dead.
Our love has gone so far away that it can never come back.
I'll never be able to say I love you because you're gone.
You'll always be out of the bay and far from my love.

You Are Lost

You are lost.
Lost in your own world and no longer know my name.
You no longer remember of this place where I gave you my love.
You are lost in love and lost in a place of your own with no return.
You've left me here to cry and think about today and tomorrow.
You used to ask me questions like you really cared for me.
You'd ask me about our love and I thought forever the days would go by without a single worry.
My love for you lives on, but do you still feel the same like the first time?
Do you still love me the way you had when you first said I was your angel?
You're a knife that stabs into me that hurts badly, but I can't turn away.
I can't run away from your love because I love you too much.
You kill me with your passion and then your neglect.
What do I have to do or say to take your heart back?
What can I do to take you out from your timeless world?
What do I have to say to make you love me once again?
You are lost in your own world while I am lost in my own misery.

You Melt My Heart

Could you spare one moment?
Could you spare just one little smile for me?
I don't know how but you melt my heart when you look at me.
You melt my love when I stare into those eyes and forget all the pain out there.
Your eyes take my breath away and your lips caress me even without touching me.
I'm not asking much from you at all.
I just need one moment with you.
We could be together one minute and that's enough for me.
If I have a chance to be close to you I'd be very happy.
I'll be happy to be near you and to hold you close.
One minute could last a very long time when we're together.
I'd make that one minute last for eternity.
You need to just give me that one moment, that one chance to be with you.
You'd see it's worth it.
I'd make it go forever and ever.
I'd make it last forever as long as you melt my heart with your face.

Your Love, My Love

I didn't know what we had in common or what I had that you really wanted and loved.
What did I have for you to love me?
You looked into my eyes and told me how much you cared, and that your love wasn't a game.
I thought you loved me because of who I was.
I was shy and quiet.
I never saw myself as being what you'd wanted, but still, you told me you loved me.
I believed in those words even when you walked off and left me empty because I still loved you.
I realize soon after that we had different ideas on how our love was.
For you, love was when you felt lonely and needed someone to fill your emptiness.
For me, love was from the heart, tears, and passion.
Your love, my love, they were both so different even though I tried hard to lie to myself that you loved me.
I loved you with all the seasons and showed you my deepest thoughts and feelings.
But they weren't enough, they were never enough, and they were never what you wanted or needed.
Not that I know what you really needed.

Youth, Beauty, All Gone

One minute love was blossoming, and the next, love was falling apart.
No matter what we did or said, time went by and we grew older.
I was growing old when it came to love and that made you turned away.
You left me with the lonely hours.
Everything died and the sweet words melted in my hands.
I didn't know why you had to go even though we had everything together.
You promised to love and cherish me, but those promises you failed to keep.
When time grew old, you walked away as you grew tired of my love.
You stepped out of my world and never looked back.
Youth, beauty, they were all gone in the dark of the night.
You walked away with everything I gave you emotionally.
Even though I loved you with all my heart, it wasn't enough.
When beauty died, when my youth died, everything went with them.

MUSIC
MELODIES OF LOVE

A Fool In Love

I had never loved anyone like I loved you.
Before you came into my life, I never had so many hopes and dreams for anyone or anything.
You lifted me up and were there along the way of happiness.
You were there when I was down and when I needed someone to talk to.
I loved you so much.
We used to sit and listen to the music.
The songs we listened to, you dedicated them to me.
Our lives were perfect, and you gave me everything and never let me felt lonely.
When I was in pain you were the one who loved me just right and with the kind of love I wanted.
Now, I sit here in the dark and cold empty room listening to the music and to the songs alone.
I cry for yesterday and cry because I'm a fool in loving you.
A fool in love now that you've walked away before the songs are finish and before the night is over.
A fool in love to not know the reality of loving you.
Know the pain of lies and feel the lies that kill you.
I have the pain that pierces through my gentle heart when one day you came into my life with full of happiness and the next you walked away and left sadness behind.

A Song For Our Love

In life, who doesn't have heartbreaks?
In life, who doesn't have that very first time when you sit together with your love and listen to that wonderful love song on the radio?
Who doesn't have that one time when your love misses your meeting time and you're standing there waiting in frustration?
Everyone has them, and sometimes, it turns out bad.
For us, the love songs on the radio were special during those nights when we were far.
We sat in one place listening to those sweet melodies and thinking about each other.
Those love songs were our love life and were memories I could never forget.
I guess saying goodbye is never easy especially when there are so many memories and dreams in our love.
But all dreams and memories must die.
No love songs last forever and no one can see tomorrow now that our love has ended.
The melodies have died with it.
I want to sing a song for our love, but whenever I do sing, I can't seem to find any words in my head because our love was never a love song.
I want to find the right love song for us but there isn't any out there.
The love songs we listened together now vanish into the wind.
The lyrics talk about love but our love is nothing like the love songs.

Afternoon Of Love

The voice singing in the afternoon and the voice singing me to sleep on those beautiful summer afternoon.
The voice of my heart and love now sits still in the silence of the afternoon as the sun shines down.
The quietness of those afternoons without love now creeps up on me.
The quiet footsteps pacing along the streets, they were so beautiful when you came into my life.
Those beautiful warm summer days, hand in hand, walking along the roads, they bring up so much love, but now you're nowhere near.
The passing memories like those cars passing by, never knowing where to go and never knowing when to stop, they've now slowly died away.
The passing days without you beside me, what will life be like?
What will tomorrow end with when there's no one near me but only my heart?
What will there be in life when I can never look you in your eyes and tell you how much I love you every morning waking up?

All That's Left

One small mistake and now we're apart.
One little lie and now you say goodbye.
It wasn't my fault that I gave you all my love.
It wasn't foolishness when I looked into your tender eyes and told you I loved you.
It wasn't my fault you were the only one who really brought the word joy into my life.
All that's left now is a little memory of us like the shadows we left on those walls.
Nights we walked home together and you sang to me.
Now, nights come and I'm walking home alone.
All that's left are lyrics to our love songs.
The melodies have died like the end of the world.
All that we wanted to say you've taken away.
Nothing is left here but the knocking on the door on those warm days when you came into my life.
I can always sing the love songs to myself but they will never sound the same like when you sang them to me.
All that's left in my heart is a memory of yesterday.

Before You Say Goodbye

Before you say goodbye, look into my eyes and tell me you love me.
Just one word of love even though it might forever remain in my heart and killing me softly throughout the rest of my life when I stand under the moon thinking about you.
Before you say goodbye, sing me a song, any song.
A song that'll remind me of your voice, a voice I've loved and will always love.
When the radio goes on and I hear someone sings, I'll think the voice belongs to you.
Before you say goodbye, take a look at me and look deep into my heart.
See how much you've hurt me and how much you've placed on my hands, and now you just take them away.
You take them away from my heart and take your hands away from mine leaving me here fulfilling my dreams alone.
Say goodbye with a kiss and a word of love even if you never come back tomorrow.
I want you to kiss me one last time.
After you leave, I want to see you above the sky each night under the moon smiling down at me even if it'll remind me of you.

Music ~ Melodies Of Love

Breath of Love

I want to hear you breathe and hear your voice when you call me over.
I want to hear you sing and listen closely when you speak to me.
I want to see your lips move, want to kiss you, and feel you one last time before the sun sets over the horizon.
I want to touch you one last time before I step back away from you.
Once last touch before you shut the door and leave me hanging on the edge of the mountain.
I want to touch your hands and touch those lips before daylight ends and I'm all alone.
Breath of love, the love you give to me in the morning, at night, and whenever you're next to me, just breathe.
Breathe the air, the love that surrounds me, that gives me sensational feeling whenever you're next to me.
I want to live that moment before the sun sets in the horizon.
I want to live that moment before daylight ends and you leave me on top of the world singing the love songs all alone.

Cold Nights

Close the windows, pull down the curtains, and pull up the sheets because it'll be another night without you like those many cold nights before we met.
Close the door and shut the world away from this emptiness inside.
Sit and listen to the love songs that once were sweet and they were the words that spoke to me about you.
Those words were everything to my life.
Today, everything has turned cold.
Even the sweet words have now turned sour and the sounds of love now break my heart.
I sit here looking at the lights above the ceiling on a cold summer night thinking about love.
I sit here thinking about the misery I'll go through from now until the end of time living without you.
The cold nights and dim lights from the living room are all that's left of my memories of you.
The sofas, the bed, and the telephone; they're all so empty like I've never seen before.
Cold nights, not even the pillows and blanket can keep me warm when I'm without you.
I sit and look at the clock and watch as the hands move back and forth on those twelve numbers.
I look and think about when the time will stop and you'll come back to me.

Crying Is Just More Pain

The day you left everything seemed fine.
I held on to the poems you gave me and held on to everything that was yesterday.
I was very happy, though, I was living in misery.
Today, I don't want to think about yesterday or want to know about tomorrow.
One thing I do know and that is I'll always love you.
I've realized crying is just more pain and have found that love is just a game.
I cry and laugh, but I live happier without you.
I sing the song of love like reading a book because once it's finished, it's all in history.
Crying is just more pain and loving is even more pain.
Nothing lives without pain and nothing is happier than when you're in love, but nothing is sadder than when you fall apart.
I'll be happy without you like two birds ready to fly into the freedom sky.
I'll never call you or be sad again.
Without you here, forever I'm happy alone knowing yesterday is gone.

Crying Shoulder

Where will I find the long lost love I've searched for all these years?
Where will I find the long lost kiss that was on my lips once but now have disappeared?
The love has gone away with the wind and now the tears are building up.
Now, I need a crying shoulder and want my tears to fall down my cheeks.
I want you to see what your love has done to me and what your heart has left upon me.
There's nothing left of me but an empty mind.
I can't think, can't tell what day or what time is it, and can't do anything anymore.
Crying shoulder, where have you gone to when I need you most?
What has God done to our love?
What have I done to deserve this pain?
The world of love under the bright sunlight when the blue sky seemed to be walking with us wherever we went.
The voice that made the birds flew into our arms in those warm summer nights. Where are they?
When you sang your verses you made my heart fell from my chest to my feet.
I want to hear your voice and want to feel the pain one more time.
I want to walk my way without thinking about you and want to hear the rain.
I want to close my ears to block the pain and block the heartbreak I'm feeling right now.

Daydreaming

Each tear, each love song, and each of the laughter; you were always there to share them with me.
You walked me through the pain, the joy, and the happy evenings when we were together in those restaurants and museums.
Today, they've all dissolved like my dreams.
Each tear, as I remember, you gave them all to me.
When you took me in your warm arms and up into the bed.
When you told me tales and jokes, they made me laugh.
Those tears were tears of joy, but today, there are no more stories and no more tales to tell.
These tears, they're not tears of joy.
Each love song, as I remember, you gave them all to me.
When you sang to me and I heard that soft voice I felt deep into my sleep.
You sang so smoothly and tenderly, I just loved the way you sang and loved the way the melodies flew back and forth in my heart.
Each laugh, as I remember, you gave them all to me when you said how beautiful I looked in your arms.
I laughed to feel the joy, but toda,y there's no more beauty.
No more yesterday, just me and the room.
Just me and the empty bed daydreaming about yesterday.

Even The Birds Sang

Living without you, I never thought this would become reality.
I could never have thought you'd say goodbye so quickly before the leaves turned colors.
You said goodbye before the flowers blossomed with the coming spring.
Even the birds sang when you said goodbye.
I stood there in the middle of nowhere watching as you walked down the lonely silent road.
Slowly, you disappeared and my life was all dark.
I couldn't see the morning even if the sun was shining through.
I couldn't see the lights even if the moon and the stars shined brighter than they did ever before.
I couldn't hear the voices talking to me because I was heartbroken to see you walk away.
The birds sang to me in their lonely sobbing voices.
I listened to them, felt their beating hearts, and watched as they flew away leaving me behind.
And then I remembered of you.
Why so sad?
Why so lonely?
Where's the love that I saved for the future?
Where are the lips I kissed so many nights?
So many afternoons together, where are you?
Can you hear the birds singing so sad and lonely right now?
Can you hear me calling your name?

For The One Who Said Goodbye (480th Poem)

If time could be stopped and I could stay young forever, would you love me more?
If I could give you all my life, would you love me more than ever?
I could climb the highest mountain, swim the longest ocean, and sing to you all your favorite songs; would you look at me more romantically?
If I do whatever you say, would you come back and love me with all your heart?
I don't know why it hurts so much to love you, but I'd forget all the pain just to have you back in my arms.
For the one who said goodbye, come back through our love songs.
For the one who said goodbye, come back and relive yesterday.
Open your arms to hold me tight.
Please don't go, don't leave me again, and don't tell me anymore lies.
Don't let the minutes pass by without loving me.
I need your love, so come back and love me again.
Come back to me and tell me tomorrow you'll be there with me forever.

For You I Write

When I met you I fell in love with you right away.
You made me laugh and every single word you said made me smile with joy.
With every touch you warmed me with care.
With your love, I didn't think of anyone else.
For you, I sang the love songs.
They were the songs that made us happy, that made us stayed together.
For you, I forgot the pain and sorrow and loved you with all my life.
I did everything for you to be happy.
Now, you've gone away and forgotten about me and the times when we spent together.
You've even forgotten the songs I sang to you.
Nothing I did made you happy, nothing I did made you think twice about not leaving.
For you I write, I write in tears of all the memories we've had together.
I put them in words, write them up as a poem, and put them into melodies to write a love, or should I say, a heartbreak song dedicated to you.
For you I write, I write with sorrows and lost, the pain you've left here with me.
For you I write, for you, I've done everything, but they didn't make you happy.
You were never happy being with me.

Forgetting Is Remembering

Myfriends told me if dreams aren't meant to be then forget them.
All of my friends tried to comfort me to make me forget about you, but no matter what they or I did, you were all over my mind.
Whenever I heard the songs on the radio I remembered of those days together. How could I ever forget them?
Even through the sadness and pain of losing you I tried to be happy and tried to keep those memories last forever.
But reality was always sadder and more painful than dreams.
Forgetting you was all about remembering because when I closed my eyes to sleep I saw you running to me.
I held out my arms to embrace you, but just before I could, reality once again took you away.
I found the sunlight before my face and another day had begun.
I wanted to cry to forget all over again but I couldn't because I could never forget you.
My friends told me to let go of those memories and begin anew, but whenever I found someone new, the person just reminded me of you.
Within the new happiness I found an old sadness.
Forgetting was remembering, and remembering was hurting.

Give Me One More Chance

Give me one more chance, just one more chance to relive that one day before you leave me.
Give me one more chance, just one more look at your face, just one for chance to hold you in my arms and hear your heart beats one last time.
If only I could hear you say you love me one last time then I can let you go forever.
Give me one more chance to say I'm sorry, sorry for all the heartbreaking moments I had brought into your life.
Say I'm sorry for all the moments I couldn't be there to love and hold you.
Give me one more chance to listen to you speak and hear the words that I couldn't hear through the many hours I wasn't there.
Let me sing to you one last time so forever I can let you go.
Sing to you the love songs I could never sing to you again.
Sing to you the songs you wanted to hear when you were still here with me.
Just give me one last chance to say all I have to say and forever you can leave this place.
One last time to hear me say goodbye, goodnight, and good morning.
Just one last chance to say all that I have to tell you and forever I can die in love.

Got To Hold On

Sing me the songs like you used to do when we lied in bed and listened to the radio.
Sing them like you used to when the night was still warm and dreamy.
Sing me the songs you once jokingly said you'd written for me.
I want to be happy at this very moment but you're gone.
I want to sing the songs and want you to come and hear me sing because the songs don't sound the same without you.
Perhaps, it'd be better for you to sing to me so I could hear the voice that caressed me through those empty hours.
I know I've got to hold on to those moments.
I've got to hold on to those kisses, and keep those nights and hours when you walked with me in my heart.
Hold on to all of them because I could never relive them again.
Hold on to your heart even though you're not here anymore.
You'll never come back nor will I ever hear you sing the songs again.
I'll never hear your voice, never see you walk into my arms, and never feel you again.
What more to say?
What's left to sing?
Nothing here but an empty bed and empty room.
Nothing but the end of the love songs you used to sing for me.

Music ~ Melodies Of Love

Heartbroken

Is there a better place to be right now than to be home listening to the crickets outside the windows?
Is there a better place to be right now than in the bed?
Close my eyes and fall into a deep sleep to forget about the days and nights, and to forget about you.
Heartbroken, nothing better than falling asleep to forget.
Forget your lies, forget how you'd told me you never loved me, and forget the way you looked at me when you left.
I want to forget and want to leave this world.
Just close my eyes and fall asleep to stop the heart from beating.
I block my ears from hearing the sounds that are so much like your voice.
I block them away like when you sing those lovely songs to me.
They sounded so tenderly, yet now kill and hurt me.
I don't want to hear the waves hitting against the sand or the birds chirping outside.
I don't want to see my face and don't want to see you or anything that has to do with you.
I want to block away the world to stop the pain in my heart.
I want my heart to stop beating to stop the bleeding from your words and lies.

Hearts Beating

As I close my eyes I feel you coming to me.
I feel you breathing into my face but when I open my eyes you're never there.
You never come when I need you most and never say a word to me when we're alone in our room.
You never look at me nor do you say you love me.
You don't have what you used to have when we first met.
I remember you used to talk a lot and made me laugh.
We had so much fun together through those many laughs whenever we walked outside in those beautiful spring days.
What have happened to you?
Is it me who has turned you into this uncaring person?
Why do you not talk to me?
Why do you not see me the way you used to?
What has happened to your touch?
What has happened to those golden words and special moments whenever we were alone in our world?
What has happened to all the tender calls and the loving sounds of our beating hearts?
I still feel our hearts beating next to each other like when we lay in this bed at night and you kissed me.
I feel your heart right here but it's only a false memory because you're not here like those nights ago.

Lonely, I Sing

Lonely, I sing the song as I walk down the road that was once bright.
I walk this road that was once full of colors and dreams.
This road once covered the laughter of happiness when one heart collided with another.
I sing because the birds are singing to the arrival of spring.
Flowers are growing vividly with the feel of spring.
Here, the roses bloom red like my heart, but they're happier than me with the arrival of spring.
Spring no longer has any meaning at all for me because it represents you.
You brought sunlight to my life one beautiful spring day but then you died with spring when you went away.
Why did you leave with spring?
Why couldn't you stay with me?
Why did you go and left me with summer?
I'm like a flower right now, and even though spring is here, I'm fading away with the summer sun instead of blossoming.
I sit here like a rose's pedals drifting slowly away onto the grass with the days gone by.
I sit and wonder why the wind is so cruel when it's so warm and so beautiful outside.

Losing Love

When you took my hands into yours and turned on our favorite song, and we danced, I knew right then it was the end of our love.
You'd decided to go and abandoned our love.
When you opened the door and said goodbye, I sat in the room as the music continued playing.
I listened to the song while in pain and filled with tears.
The pain in losing love, losing the one you've been with for so many years, it was unbearable.
When the song stopped playing, it was all over for us.
The door was shut, and forever, we could never go back again.
You'd forgotten the hair, eyes, and face you'd spent so many wonderful nights with.
You no longer wanted to remember of them.
Losing love is pain, living with you was the best, but it was also the worst.
But time will change and hair will turn gray.
Love must go on and it must die because love cannot stop time, and for sure, time is a pain in love.

Love Has Faded Away

Let's dance together one last time before the morning takes you away.
Hold me tight and don't let go of this one special night.
Look into my eyes as if you still love me.
I know when the sun rises I'll lose you forever.
I'll watch the days together with you burn out like the candles.
I'll close my eyes and listen to your heart beats close to mine.
I'll smile through the falling tears and dance to the love song playing in the background.
When the music stops, my heart will too because I'll have to say goodbye to you.
Love has faded away when I can no longer feel your heart beating next to mine.
Love has faded away when I can no longer hear you breathing next to me.
For now, pretend tomorrow will never come.
I know in my heart I can replay the music and dance with you forever to make you stay.
But I also know I can't stop the sun from rising.
I can't stop you from going because our love has faded away even before the sun has risen.
I can say I love you to make you stay at the morning light but it won't make any different by the looks of your eyes.

Music ~ Melodies Of Love

Love In My Heart (400th Poem)

It was only yesterday when you came knocking on my door.
It was only yesterday when we walked together hand in hand.
I could hear you singing that special love song to me.
It was only yesterday I was so happy in love.
It was only yesterday that my heart was full of life when love was there with me.
The songs on the radio played softly as we sat together.
We laughed and kissed, and everything seemed fine.
I could never have thought it'd ever ended.
One day I came home and found you gone.
I looked and looked but couldn't find you.
I listened to the love songs on the radio over and over trying to understand why youdd left.
Life was empty, nothing was the same, and no one was there to answer my calls.
I wanted to leave and go far away to a place where I'd be happy without remembering about your love.
But no matter what I did or where I went, I had loved you too much.
All the places I went, no matter where in this world, there was nothing but you in my mind.
Your love was in my heart, and no matter how hard I tried, I couldn't find a way to let it go.

Love In No Means

When we were young I used to sing to you the songs you loved.
I sang the love songs that made us one.
I whispered to you the words and melodies you wanted to hear.
Time went by and the world moved on, and so did you.
The one who I loved left with the seasons and the songs we loved were left behind with history.
I wanted to hold on to time and the love songs, but time didn't stay.
The melodies stopped and the words died out when we said goodbye..
If I knew the future ahead of time, could I have stopped you from leaving?
Would I have wished for time to stop so you could stay with me and watch the days go by?
Loving you was in no means easy, but without you, it was even harder.
Today, I sit here and wish I could turn back the hand of time and start everything again.
I wish you could be the same person who I once loved, but that's not possible is it?
There are many things I want to get back, but when I look back, all I see is that sad moment when we departed.

Continue with "Sad With Love"

Music In The Night

I listen to the music and let my heart sinks deep into the melodies as they play.
I let myself fall into the words as if searching for something that could never be found.
I close my eyes and let the melodies take me away.
I fall deep into an eternity of sleep never having to know the heartache you've brought into my life.
I don't know why I fell in love with you.
I can't figure out why I kissed you when I should've known today was coming.
Music in the night, the melodies play on as the words come to my heart and slowly kill me.
Music in the night, I let the music takes me away into my dream to forget you've flown away like the summer wind.
The cold winter has arrived outside while I sit inside listening to the music and asking myself all these questions.
I don't want to cry but as the music plays on into the night, I'll cry.
In my heart, there're so many words I want to tell you to release this sadness. But I can't say anything since you're not here.
I want the music to set my soul free of this hurt, but as it plays on and on, all I feel is even more sadness and despair.

My Memories Of Yesterday

It hasn't been that long since we met but everything seems different today with you.
As for myself, nothing has changed.
The songs we used to sing are not here anymore.
The sweet talks and amicable conversations we once had have faded into history.
I want the happy memories but they're all gone.
We tried so hard to make each other happy but we were just growing tired of each other.
Time is passing by like the rain falling down from the sky.
Do you still remember of what we shared together?
Sometimes, I don't want to remember about yesterday because I only remember of all the happy times and forget about all the sad times we shared.
We told each other we'd wait and be together until the end of time.
Today is here but there's just a lonely space with no one here to fill.
The songs we used to sing are very different from the ones we've heard.
The promises we had are no promises anymore.
Some promises have passed by while some remain, although they aren't the same like what we used to know.
My memories of yesterday are still in my heart and I'll keep them in my heart no matter what.
What about you?
Do you cherish those memories or have you already forgotten about them?

Never Should I Cry

It feels like only yesterday when we first kissed.
Lips to lips, it feels like it'd just happened but the feeling I have is nothing more than a memory.
The love songs you sang to me and the lovely melodies I whispered in your ears are now nothing more than the air and wind that come and go.
Do you feel sad without me?
I'm here waiting and telling myself never should I cry even without you.
Do you feel what I'm feeling without your love?
I'm walking in the dark of the night knowing you're looking down, and wherever you are, that you're happy.
I'm walking along the never-ending roads and not looking back knowing very well I'll forever miss you.
Forever, we'll miss and lose each other.
No more crying and no more love to give to each other.
I'll be happy without you.
I'll laugh and smile without you here because I know these are the things you'd want me to do when you're gone.

Once You Are Gone

I remember those times when we walked this boardwalk.
We held hands, kissed, and loved every single moment that was there.
The lights along the boardwalk made it felt like a dream, like we were in a fantasy.
We were walking and making a lifetime of memories.
In my heart, I asked myself what I should do once you're gone from my life.
Now, that question has been answered.
You've left forever to a place where I'll never be able to see you again.
Can you hear me when I whsiper your name?
Do you feel my pain wherever you are right now?
You'll never come back in my arms.
I want this to be a nightmare that ends before time stops, but this is real.
Reality can never be changed.
If I'd known what I know today then I would've never let you go.
I'd hold on tight to you that night when the music was still fresh and we were still dancing.
Eyes to eyes, we were dancing on the boardwalk and people were clapping along to with our melodies.
We forgot about time while our love took us far away.
That was the moment of love and peace unlike today where the music has died and the lights have faded along the boardwalk.

Our Love Songs

You used to sing those love songs to me with your soft and tender voice during those years together.
You were my true love, but time went on and our love ended.
One distance apart we walked away from each other while the love songs remained.
Heaven cried as the rain fell continuously through the days and nights.
The light was forever gone from my life.
Life changed that very day when the only melodies that played were the rain falling outside.
Sad memories flashed by and slowly the love songs died away with all the memorable days together.
If we could go back to those days once again, would we be able to fix all our problems and continue on?
Our love songs were all I had during those days of loneliness.
I wanted your love to live forever but all I had was the music.
You said goodbye and ended the love songs.
The memories went with you and all you left behind were broken dreams and unfinished love songs.

Play The Song

Play the song one last time even if it hurts me.
Let me cry, let the tears fall to forget when spring was still beautiful before you entered my life.
Play the song, just play it one last time even if it kills me.
I want to listen to it and remember the pain you've caused.
Remembering is only pain and no love, but forgetting is even more torturous to my heart.
The song that once sounded so sweet now sours out like a bad dream.
There're no melodies but just words coming into my head and piercing my heart.
I want to hear you play the song one last time even if the song hurts me deep inside.
Play the song to let me know that you're still around.
Let me forget you like I've forgotten about the song.
Play it like the knife that pierces through my heart, wounding and killing me as I sit here listening.
I sit here and watch you play and sing the song to forget about yesterday.
I want to forget through the wine.
Taste the bitterness of this drink to forget the bitterness of life without you.
I listen to the memories of yesterday and remember when I welcomed you with love during that spring afternoon full of life.

Quietness

Twelve long seasons together and they seemed like forever to me.
But for you, they meant nothing.
Twelve long seasons filled with happiness, dreams, and hopes.
Those wonderful wishes under the moonlight quickly faded away like the moon and stars.
I sat in the quietness of my room waiting for your footsteps.
I hoped you'd come back to yesterday memories, but all I heard was the silence of my loneliness.
All I saw was my shadow fading with time on the cold walls.
Just a lonely shadow fading in the quietness of the daylight.
I loved you with all my tears and loved you with all my life.
I had nothing to lift me up when you left.
I loved you in those heartbreaking moments and through those sorrowful years.
I loved you through the wine and music, but they weren't enough for you.
Nothing was enough, and nothing that I gave made you stay.
Nothing at all.

Right Here Waiting

One day the sun shined bright, the water flowed, and the flowers blossomed.
One day I sat and waited for my lover's footsteps to come and take me away.
I waited as the hours went by.
My hair turned gray, my eyes were filled of tears, and my heart was dead.
The tears fell like the rain outside.
I sang one song after another trying to forget the passing time, but it didn't work.
As time went on it made me more and more aware of the love I no longer have.
Today, I still wait for that someone to come and take me away.
I'm right here waiting for the new song to play and for my love to sing to me.
I'm waiting for time to stop and for the seasons to go on because when they do my love will come.
My love has promised that she'll come back ,and my heart has waited ever since.
My heart will wait even if these tears continue to fall and my dreams never come.
I'll be right here waiting for her to come and walk with me through the long beautiful life.
I'll wait through the seasons as the rain comes, the leaves fall, and the snow melt away into the sunlight.
I'll sing the love song to keep my heart beating.
I'll wait through the hours as the sun fades away and the stars shine down on my way home.
The wind will whisper to me one word after another, and in my desperation, I'll pretend it's my lover telling me she's coming home.

Run

Run because love is coming.
Hearts will be broken and time will die.
Run because your love has changed so much.
Your love no longer belongs to me but to someone else.
I want to run away from the pain that'll come in the near future.
What's left for us when I have nothing for you and you have nothing for me?
We walk our separate ways and our love only has what we're having right now and nothing more.
I'll cry for us and miss your love, but there's nothing we can do to change what's here.
There's nothing we can do to change what we're feeling right at this moment.
Don't feel sorry but instead just live with what there is.
We can run and hide from the pain but I'll be the one with the most tears to cry.
You'll have someone else to hold and love.
I'll have no one, not even a piece of yesterday memory to keep.
No one will hold me in the lonely nights and no one will sing to me.
I'll run far way and never stop to look back at those old days.

Sad With Love

When we were young I used to sit and listen as you sang to me.
There was so much you had in your heart for me in the looks of your eyes.
The melodies and songs played in my head when I was alone.
Time flew by and things changed.
You left me with a broken heart and left with me all the memories of our youths.
The songs remained in my hearts but we couldn't go back to where we started.
Today, I sing those songs to remind myself of those youthful days long gone.
I wonder where you are now and wonder about what you're doing.
Do you still think about me and all that we shared?
Or has time erased your memories of those younger days?
What I left behind I could never replace.
The love's gone but the memories remain.
Now the music plays and I sign the songs to think about yesterday.
The sadness fills my heart as I remember of our long lost love.
The years are still young and the days are still bright, but the eyes that looked deep into mine are gone.
I'm sad with love, sad with time, but most importantly, I'm sad when yesterday comes back through the songs we used to sing together.

Silent Music

The music plays on even though you've gone.
I can't hear the words or notes playing as my head wonders to another place.
The music plays on but all I hear is my dying heart beating slowly.
The melodies sink deep into my mind as the torrential rain fall outside.
The music plays as the lights shine and dim.
Silently, I watch the hours go by and slowly melt away like the winter snow.
The music plays on while I sit in the stillness of the night.
In the silence of the night I listen to the crying of the lonely heart.
I watch as the rain falls and disappears onto the ground before my eyes.
There's nothing here in my eyes but falling tears.
The music plays on loudly but I hear nothing but the silence.
I feel nothing but the dying heart of yesterday happiness.
It's the happiness of when you were here in this room listening to the melodies with me on the radio.
The beautiful melodies that swept our hearts and love into a beautiful dream.
You were here with me listening to the silent music of the night.

Sing For The Lonely Hearts

Sing for the lonely hearts that are like mine when she walked away with the songs she'd written for me.
Sing for the lonely hearts that are broken when the melodies she'd written for me set my heart ablaze.
Sing for the lonely hearts when they cry in the night to wave goodbye to the sad memories that have been put upon the heavy shoulders.
Sing for the lonely hearts when they whisper the loneliness in the night.
Through the darkness of the night I turn around and there's no one but the shadows of the night.
What does love have that can't be broken?
How long can love last?
How long can the heart go without being broken?
How long can the love songs last?
How many nights crying without love?
She says she loves you but when you close your eyes and open them, she's gone.
She says she cares about you but when love dies, she doesn't care anymore.
Sing for the lonely hearts, sing for the light in the morning when her smile brightened up my day.
Sing for the lonely hearts, sing for the happiness in the afternoon when her laughter make my heart melts away into the night.
Sing for the lonely hearts, sing one last time before the beautiful eyes disappear into the darkness of the night and I'm here alone with the emptiness.

Sing For The Lying Tears

Go ahead and cry but I won't turn around and take your hands.
I won't comfort you because those days are over.
You walked away from my love and lied to me through those happy days.
Now, there's nothing left but me.
Just walk away and take all the lies with you.
I still feel a little bit of love for you deep in my heart, but the memories you left behind still linger.
I don't want any more pain in love.
You promised me a lot but all I got were lies.
Those hurtful lying words are too familiar to me.
Don't waste those lying tears on me.
You can tell me whatever and cry all you want, but our time has gone.
Things have changed for me and I can't trust you no more.
Maybe you shouldn't have lied to me in the first place.
Now you tell me you love me but all I hear is you singing those lying tears like those many days before.

Sing For The One In My Heart

One day while I was walking home I saw you walking down the road on the other side of the street.
I wanted to say hi but I realized yesterday was gone.
So I turned and walked away because in my heart you were completely gone like the happiness you'd left behind when you said goodbye.
Perhaps, yesterday, everything we had were meant to be so today we'd meet on the street face to face, and even with all the love, there's nothing left to say to one another.
Perhaps, yesterday, those moments were all beautiful dreams that I always wanted life to turn out to be.
Today, on the street we once walked, all I could do was turn my back and walked away.
Deep in my heart, I sang the love song as we walked with our backs to each other.
I sang the song as we walked farther and farther away from each another.
I sang the song for my heart and for the one yesterday who'd walked and loved me.
Maybe I was just singing to erase the pain you'd left with me.
I wanted to glance back and take one good look at you but something in my heart told me to keep on going.
If you really wanted to talk to me you would've smiled when our eyes met.
But all I saw was the distant look in your eyes as you pretended you didn't see me.

Music ~ Melodies Of Love

Song For The Dead

There'll be a day when I die, when I close my eyes forever and the memories are locked in my heart.
All the sad songs playing in the background will sing forever goodbye.
The tears falling down won't be that of happiness, and one sad goodbye means eternity.
The words written on the stone will bring the rain.
The roads ahead will be empty because thhere won't be anyone but me.
There'll be a day when I stand alone watching the white clouds fading in the distance.
I'll look at the faces before my eyes and wonder where those days have gone to because I can no longer remember them like I used to.
There'll be a day when my hands grow tired and my feet give out.
That day will be the end of my beating heart when all the love I've given come back to me.
The years will stop moving because I'll be the one with the laughter and tears in my hands.

The End Of The Love Song

When the leaves fall outside and the warm air disappears, it'll be the end of the love song.
The leaves will drop down into my hands, the hands that have once held you tight and given you roses.
Do you remember the hands that once touched you gently with care and love?
Time has gone by and you've probably forgotten.
The past sometimes dies like the wind that goes by, like the colors that we see before we close our eyes.
All memories fade away like a dream or perhaps a nightmare.
The song that our love has turned into now slowly comes to a stop.
Our love seems to only have lasted for a few minutes like the song itself, even though we've been together for a long time.
The end of a love song comes too quickly like a story with a sad ending.
I listen to it remembering of our sad past.
I hear the voice and melodies like the voice of Celine Dion singing the Titanic's song.

The Space Between Us

Some people ask me why I walk alone in the emptiness of the night and I tell them it's the silence of the night that gives me peace.
Some people ask me why I sing the sad love songs and I tell them it's these songs that make me forget.
But I never tell them who I'm singing these songs for.
I could never tell them about the loneliness in my life.
There's a silence in this room that holds me tight and tries not to let go.
It's the place that once holds sweet memories of love, but they've all turned into snow.
They're melting like the sound of the sad love songs I sing.
Some people ask me why I look to the stars and whisper to myself.
I tell them I whisper for the nights to never go by, but I could never tell them that I wish for the nights to forever be gone.
Sometimes, I wonder if it's really the nights that keep me company or whether they're what keeping me from forgetting about this person.
There's a space between us that I want to let go, but somewhere deep, I still hold on.
I hold on to the nights and wish they never go by.
Maybe deep inside I still love this person like when this person had also loved me too.

Those Days, My Love

Yesterday, we were walking down this road with the sky so blue and life so beautiful.
I thought it was a dream with music playing in my heart like your heart next to my ear.
For you, I gave everything in my heart.
When the saddest moment came into my life your smile was all I needed to forget the pain.
The happiness was so deep those days while in love.
Your laughter was all that surrounded me.
Your love and tenderness calmed my soul and mind.
I was so much in love with you, how could you've walked away?
I told myself no matter what happened in the future, you'd always be the one and the only one I love.
No matter what happened tomorrow, you'd always be the love of my life.
Those days, my love, I gave you everything because you said you'd love me until the end of time.
Those days, my love, you kissed me and turned the night into a magical dream.
Those days, my love, you said I was your everything.

Tonight, The Last Night

You came and gave me one beautiful dream that I held on tightly.
It was one dream with love and care, and it gave me a smile on my face whenever I think about it.
You came into my dream like a light shining a path for me.
You were there one moment but the next, the light faded and you were gone.
The bed was empty like before I met you.
The laughter in the room dissipated like a storm that comes and goes whenever it wants to.
You were there one moment laughing with me and singing the love songs, and the next, you were nowhere to be found.
I laughed to myself and sang alone into the endless dream.
I laughed with the tears of pain instead of the happiness I once had.
I hoped to see you once again in my dreams.
I wanted to love you again, but how could I?
What you'd left behind still remained in my heart.
Day after day, the love and memories only brought me sadness.

Vivid Thoughts

I miss you so much that my head hurts.
I miss the kisses and those dreamy eyes that once looked deep into my soul and caught my love like no others had done before.
I miss the voice that once called me in the night.
You were next to me telling me how lovely I looked that night.
I took your hands under the moonlight as the music playe under the candlelight.
I told you I loved you and that moment was forever imprinted in my memory.
You were here then but now you're not, and the thought of you leaving hurts so much.
The thought of never seeing you again has consumed my mind.
I still keep to my promise of loving you, but where are you?
Do you know how much pain I'm in without you singing the love songs?
Don't you want to come back and spend the rest of your life with me?
I was the one you said you loved the most and the one you shared your secrets with.
Now, am I not the one who you miss the most?

Voice Of Yesterday

Goodbye will be the last word I'll be hearing from you.
Goodbye will be the last time I'll hear your voice.
From today onward I'll regard your voice as the voice of yesterday.
Goodbye will be the last time I'll hear you say any words to me.
This will be the last time I'll look you in the eyes before you go.
Where're you going?
Why do you want to go?
Why don't you want to stay and be together?
Why do you want to go when the sun hasn't set in our love?
The voice of yesterday, I'll always remember your voice.
I'll never forget the moment you first spoke to me nor the first time you sang to me, even though they're all gone now.
From this moment on remembering of your voice will be the only choice I have left.
Nothing with you and nothing left without the voice of love.
It was the voice that loved me so much.
Now, you slowly fade away and all I hear is the echoing of your voice slowly bouncing off somewhere so far.

Voices In The Night

When I close my eyes I can feel you beside me like those winter nights when love was with us.
I feel you like when I still knew what love felt like and what passion really was.
With you, I've learned how hard life can be without the person who you've loved for so many nights and days.
I can't sleep without you and the warmth that you've brought into my life.
Every time I close my eyes I hear voices in the night that talk to me like the many words you said when you lay down next to me.
I can still feel the warmth and the heat just like those nights when you closed your eyes and went deep into your sleep.
I watched you sleep and listened to you breathe.
I enjoyed and loved that moment so much that I couldn't imagine my life without you.
But time passed by and you went with it when you decided to leave me.
Time didn't stay forever and that was the same for you.
The voices of the night called and took you away leaving me here thinking.
Now I cry to myself on my pillows.
Only the pillows know the pain I'm going through.
No one else knows and cares anymore.

When Dreams Come True

I know I won't be able to see you again or hear you call my name.
I won't be able to hear you breathe in the night when I lie down to sleep.
You'll only be in my dreams in the lonely nights when I close my eyes.
You'd be there lying down next to me keeping me safe and warm from all the coldness of the night.
My dreams will bring you back like bringing back the happiness that was here when you still loved me.
When dreams come true, it'll be the day you come home.
When dreams come true, those sweetest days will come back and the sadness will go away.
You'll be with love, and those tender eyes will look deep into mine as I fall into your arms.
You'll hug and kiss me like the good old days when the songs were playing and we danced through the night.
We'll listen to the music and dance all over again through the everlasting melodies.
When dreams come true, love will be beautiful and we'll fall in love all over again.

When Tomorrow Never Comes

We used to wonder when the love song would end and when we'd go our separates ways.
I thought we could really work it out and try harder to keep our love alive but I was thinking way too much.
I wanted our love to survive because I thought love existed between you and I.
But in the end, all my hopes were dashed when you ended everything.
You wanted to go and there was nothing I could've said to make you stay.
Today, the love remains and I wish tomorrow would never come because everyday without you is a sorrow I have to live with.
When tomorrow never comes, I'll think of you and the sweet moment when we were still in love.
When tomorrow never comes, I'll sit and count the lonely days.
I'll wait for the heartbreak love songs to come on the radio while I think about you and the good old days when love songs flourished.
The night comes and I feel the loneliness whispering to me as it tries to strangle my memories of yesterday.
I look up into the stars and wish for you to come back instantly.
I hope for the door to burst open and there you stand smiling at me.
But all I see are the tree branches moving with the wind as the wind whispers its sadness to me.

When Will Love Come To Me?

I've waited all my life for someone to come and share the lonely nights with me.
I wait and wait, but there's never anyone.
When will love come to me?
When will someone sing the love songs for me?
When will someone hold me so that the lonely days can vanish into thin air?
Many times in my sleep I've dreamed of someone special who makes me laugh.
I dream we're walking down the river with the moon and stars smiling down on us.
We'd kiss and spend hours holding each other.
And like always, when I wake from my dreams, they just make me cry.
There're so many tears when I wake up knowing there's no one beside me.
There's no happiness without that special love.
When will love come to me?
Why must there be so many hours, days, and nights waiting?
Where are you and why won't you come to take this loneliness away?

Who'll Be There When You're Gone?

I told you I was fine and understood what you were saying when you told me the other person had more to offer you.
I watched you go as the moon and stars disappeared into the night.
You walked away like the water flowing in the creek.
I could try to hold onto you, but like the water, you'll pass through my hands.
My friends asked me if I was okay and all I could do was lie.
I told them anything so it wouldn't worry them, but they saw through me because heartbreak is stronger than lies.
My tears were all I had to show as I cried for tomorrow without you.
I saw before my eyes the bouquet being thrown into the air but I'm not the one beside you.
I wasn't the person in your arms dancing on the dance floor.
The dance continued and I saw myself dancing with my own shadow.
The wedding songs played through my ears.
They were the songs I'd picked for our weddings.
Yet, all was gone because I wasn't the one kissing you.

Part 3: *Snow Falling In June*

Xena

Xena, if only you could be the arms that caress me through the time of pain.
Can you be the wings that fly me through the nights and the voice that sings to me?
Xena, I think about you when I sit in the café drinking the cold coffee that's plain and bitter like your love for me.
What has time done to me now that I'm here without you?
What have I done to deserve this coldness from you?
Xena, if only you could be the river that flows me to your heart.
Take me to where you are to ease these falling tears when I think about you holding and kissing me.
Sing to me the songs that'll take me to where you are so we could love again.
Dance with me and forget about the rest of the world.
Just the two of us dancing the night away with the melodies I've written for you.
Dance with me so I can forget all about the loneliness you've left behind.
Dance with me for the last time as the wind of spring caresses our bodies.
Dance so when I die I can still tell the tale of my life and the tale of loving you.
Xena, tell me you love me one last time even though by the looks of your eyes, your love no longer belongs to me.

DREAM
Living Out of Reality

Don't Leave Me

What can I say so you won't stop loving me?
What will I do when you decide our love should end?
Where can I go to stop my heart from bleeding?
There're no words to explain how I feel at this moment.
There's nowhere to go to relive the happiness with you.
Dreams are over and reality is here, but I never thought this day would come so soon and so suddenly.
I never could've seen this day when my heart would break when I think about you.
I think about how the day would go on when you step out the door.
Don't leave me, that's all I can say right now.
Don't leave me, don't let me stay here counting each seconds without you.
Without your love, I can't think or dream.
I know your heart has changed but I need your presence.
I can't see the day without you and can't see the night without your love.
Stay with me, don't leave me.
Don't leave me here in the coldness of the night.
Stay here with me and don't leave me with this emptiness.

Don't Say You Love Me

Don't say you love me because you want to make me happy.
Don't say you love me because you want to lie to me.
Tell me you love me when you truly do.
When you look at me I see nothing in your eyes.
I want to trust every word you tell me and want to love you, but I know we both love each other in a different way.
The way you love me could never be the way I love you because the words you tell me come slowly but exit quickly.
I'm just someone in your game of love so you could come by when you're lonely.
I don't want to give you everything because I can't trust you.
You tell me you love me today and tomorrow you tell someone else the same lies.
I can't put my hopes and dreams into your lies because this will never work.
If I give everything to you then tomorrow I might end up being the only one shredding the tears.
If I give you too much then I'll get nothing back.
You could tell me you love me or hold me close.
You could even hold my hands with all your power.
In the end of the day, I could look into your eyes and not find the real love I need.
Don't say you love me because you use the same words with every other person you know.
Don't say you love me only so you could find someone to be with in the lonely hours.

Dreaming For What?

Dreaming for what when reality is truly here before my eyes.
I dream of you walking with me on the bridge as we walk under the rain holding the umbrella.
The clouds then roll by and the rain stops.
The sun appears before the clouds as I look over for your smile but all I see is the rain on the ground.
The smiles and the laughter quickly dissapate into the the wind.
No more laughter, only the sounds of someone crying in the distance.
Only the sounds of someone sobbing ahead in my darkest dreams.
Dreaming for what when tomorrow could never be what I want.
Dream of my love and dream away the pain that never could be erased from this lonely mind.
When I put out my hands for you to grab them, you're gone.
Your hands are not with mine.
No one grabs mine and no one holds me.
Dream, my love, dream of me when the rain begins outside your windows in the darkness of the night.
When you hear the raindrops falling, dream of me.
The rain will be the tears that fall gently down on my cheeks.

Dream ~ Living Out Of Reality

Dreams Gone Out Of Our Hands

The dreams we had when we held each other tight under the full moon and we kissed.
The dreams we shared between the two of us were meant to last a lifetime.
Those dreams still live in me like the memories from yesterday.
When you came into my life, you guided me through the lonely days.
Today, the footsteps we left on the winter snow remian fresh off the grounds we once walked on.
The tracks that led us home are still with me, but for you, they've disappeared.
When our dreams died, I died with them.
The moment when you walked away destroyed all the dreams we had.
The footsteps of yesterday stopped dead on their way.
Everything in my life went with you but the heartbreak.
The wind and rain swept away the memories of those happy days when we were still together.
The dreams were gone out of our hands and there were no more hoping and wishing for each other upon the happy days of tomorrow.
You walked away with nothing left but the tears in the empty dream.

Dying Dreams

Reach out your hands, can you feel my heart beating faster than it's ever been before?
Reach out your hands, can you feel my hands are cold and dried like the autumn leaves?
Reach out your hands, can you feel me breathing?
I can't feel you anywhere near me.
Laugh, just laugh in front of me so I can see it one more time before you close the door and walk away like the cool wind in the summer day.
Smile once more to let me be happy and the rest of my life I'll live in misery without your smile.
Dying dreams, even when I close my eyes to sleep at night I won't be able to hear you laugh anymore.
I can dream of the beautiful face and see those lips that whisper to me, but I'll never touch them.
I'll never feel what I used to when I was with you because they're only dreams.
They're my dying dreams with you.
Even when you come close to me, when you kiss and hug me tight in your arms, I'll never really feel them.
I'll never be able to feel the real love and arms around my body because in my dreams everything isn't real.
They're only dreams, my dying dreams of you.

Even Good Dreams Fly

I'm here waiting for you days and nights, morning and evening, but you're never here.
I sit and wait but you never show up when the sun rises and sets.
You don't come when the moon and stars shine above the night sky.
I give you all my love and trust, and give you everything important in my life.
I don't ask much from you, but one night of love and tenderness and forever you're gone.
You don't know my pain and the tears of heartbreak you give me.
My friends always tell me even good dreams fly away, but I never believe these words.
In loving you, I try to live our wonderful dreams.
I want us to have everything, I want the best in our lives, and most importantly, I want you to truly love me.
On the contrary, you never want anything to come out of our love.
All you want to do is enjoy the tender nights when you're feeling lonely.
You come with your own fulfillment and leave me behind with all the heartbreak.
I guess all good dreams do fly away.
Still, I dream about and love you regardless of the heartbreak.
I think about you regardless of the pain knowing you don't really love me.

Everything Is Forgiven

You might not realize it, but I've forgiven you.
I've forgiven you for all the heartbreak you brought.
I've forgiven you for all the sadness you brought to our love.
All I know right now is I love you.
I want you to come back because I can't live without you.
Come back to me with the memories of those happy days.
Forget the heartbreak, leave them behind and come back to my love.
Come back to yesterday when there were no tears and fights.
Live with the yesterday that'd given us dreams and a bright future ahead.
I'll be here waiting for your return.
I hope you'll come back because I love you with all my life.
Come back because I love you through all the dreams and nightmares of yesterday.
Our lives won't last forever so come back to me right at this moment.
Love me like I love you.
Love me with all your dreams and heart, and let's live forever together.

Eyes Of Pain

When I looked into your eyes I fell in love right away.
I didn't know whether I fell in love with you or because I was alone and was in need of love.
Today, I realize I'd dug deep into a love that only brought me pain.
The first moment together, I was only in need of love and you were there to fill those lonely hours.
But I soon fell deeply in love with you and couldn't let go.
I know I had many chances to end our relationship, but for some reasons I couldn't smile when I didn't see you.
Somehow, I lied to myself when I said I could make it without you.
I was wrong because your love was the eyes of pain.
I couldn't let go and couldn't stop thinking about you.
Now, I need you so much knowing there's nothing I can do to forget.
There's no one who can replace you.
Why do you bring me pain?
Why do you treat me so badly even though I put all my heart and soul into our love?
Eyes of pain, your love has never been good, but why can't I live without it?
What have you done to make me feel this way?
What have I done to deserve such misery?

Forever Is A Word

When we were together I kept on wondering what the word "forever" really meant.
When we were together everything seemed like it was a lifetime.
Nothing was going wrong, nothing was sad, and I thought forever was real.
All the stories of heartbreak and sadness in relationship, I thought I'd never have them in my life.
I was wrong, because once the love was gone, the hearts were falling apart.
The distance between us grew longer and longer as days after days and nights after nights we watched our dreams fell apart.
You no longer loved me like that day when you gave me the first kiss.
Forever was just a word.
It was just a dream or maybe a nightmare that stayed with me forever.
I didn't want to remember you and didn't want to hear the word forever anymore.
Nothing was going to be the same without your love and nothing will be forever in my life without you.

Forget Love

All the dreams from yesterday when we were hands in hands, and happiness was holding me tight.
Those sweet dreams during all the romantic nights when I didn't have to worry about being alone.
Those beautiful and careless days were filled with sweet memories as the days went by.
Today, those sweet moments linger in my mind but you're not around.
The voice that sang in the night as I dreamed away now has vanished like the wind.
The hands that held me now turn cold.
The memories of love are still in my head and so are the kisses from those soft tender lips.
The love remains within my heart but the person is gone.
No goodbye, just lots of tears falling down my face the day you left.
I don't want to be alone without your love.
I don't want to think about tomorrow, but what more is there to do at this moment?
I'll sit here trying to forget those seasons falling in love.
I'll sleep tonight trying to forget the pain you left behind.
I'll forget about tomorrow, forget those promises you made, and forget everything else so I won't have to cry when I think about you.

Forget Those Dreams

Those young loving days are over.
Sitting on the bikes and riding down the hills as we watched the sun go down up in the horizon.
You laughed with me as we held each other.
Your laughs echoed through my heart like a bulk of thunder.
I watched you smile, full of happiness, like the blue sky above during those happy summer days.
Your smiles shined like the sun giving me full of life.
I could close my eyes and forget all the sorrows, and maybe then I could be with you forever.
I could close my eyes and wish the world would stop for a brief moment so I could hear you laugh once more.
Now, there're no more dreams because they've gone from our hearts.
I stand here and watch as the sun descent slowly across the blue sky.
The birds spread their wings and fly joyfully away to another sky while I'm forever here waiting for you.
I'm locked in a memory that'll never come back.
I'm forever locked in a dream that'll never be reality.

Gentle Heart

The day you told me you loved me, I believed you.
I gave you the happiness in my life and gave you all the love in my gentle heart.
All I wished for was that you'd only tell me the truth.
The day you told me you loved me, I closed my eyes and dreamed I was in heaven.
Heaven was a paradise for you and me in my heart.
I lived a happy life thinking everyday would be like this special moment between us.
I closed my eyes to sleep and you were beside me.
When I laughed, you were there to laugh with me.
You were always there, always standing beside me making me happy.
I forgot the pain in losing love because I thought we'd be together always.
But it wasn't long before you left my gentle heart and turned my dreams into nightmares.
I fell into pieces and couldn't think straight for a second.
I went around looking for you but it seemed as though the world was empty as my heart.
I searched for you but all I found was darkness and emptiness.

Gently, You Held Me Close

Yesterday, you came to me with love.
Today, I watch you walk down the aisle with someone else.
But I'm not mad at you because I only feel sorry we've ended up like this.
I saw a better future for us and wanted to be the one next to you as we walk down the aisle.
I dreamed of the day when we stand on the dance floor and dance through the love songs we loved the most.
I told you no matter what happens in the future, I'd always be with you.
But all I can do now is watch you marry someone else.
I can do nothing more but to hide the pain in my heart.
You don't have to worry about my sadness because I truly wish you the fullest happiness with the one in your arms.
I'll be okay, and I'll forever cherish those moments we had together.
I'll remember of you in my heart, and I won't cry in front of you nor will I let you know I'm hurting inside.
I want you to see me smiling when you look at me.
I wish you'll always be happy in your life.
Don't remember of those moments when you gently held me close and kissed me goodnight.
Forget about what we had together and let me be the one who'll forever remember of those memories.
Be happy with your new love and don't remember of yesterday.
Forgot those moments we had together like the passing hours that will never come back to us.
I'll keep that moment with me forever when you gently held me close and told me we'll be together until the end of time.

Gone With Happiness

Give me back one moment to remember, to hold, and to stand beside you.
Hand in hand, let's be together like the first day.
Give me back one moment to dream with you and kiss those tender lips.
Give me one second to hear the whisper of the lonely dove.
Only one brieft second to listen to your heartbeat and forever you can walk away.
Give me one second and forever I can stand here and cry for our love.
Gone with happiness, you've taken our love with you leaving me here all empty without laughter and happiness.
You've taken everything the day you stepped out of the door.
You left behind the pain as I looked back to yesterday and hoped I could make it without you.
You left behind all the suffering while you walked away with our happiness.
You've left the daylight and taken away love.
Now, I live in darkness thinking about you and wondering about tomorrow.
I look into the horizon and wonder if the sun will ever rise again.

Have I Found The Right One?

Have I found the right one?
The one I've been searching for all my life.
The one I've had so many dreams about.
The one I've waited for in the emptiness of my lonesome existence.
I dream about love and dream of this person, but have I found the right one?
Why does it hurt so much when she looks into my eyes?
Is she the one I truly love?
Even though she hurts me I just can't stop but run into her arms.
I run into a love I don't even know if it really exists.
I run into a love that hurts so bad, but why do I love her?
Why do I think about her nights and days even though I know when she's with me she's not happy?
I'm the only one who's happy.
I'm the only person in the relationship who's enjoying the love and tender moments together.
Why am I the only one who believes in the future of our love and happiness?
So have I really found the right one?
Have I found my true love, or have I found heartbreak?

Hold On To Tonight

Last night I dreamed you came back to me.
I saw you opening the door and walked inside.
You knelled down and told me you loved me.
I was so happy I held you in my arms.
Suddenly, the lights came on and I realized it was all a dream.
I looked at the sunlight shining through the windows from the crowded world outside my bedroom and felt the sad loneliness creeping in.
The morning has only reminded me that you're gone.
It has only brought an end to my beautiful dream of you.
I wish the night would last forever so I could dream of you forever.
I wish for tomorrow to never come.
Let the darkness surrounds my life and let the silence of the night covers my room.
Let me live in a fantasy that you're still around and let me live in a world that could never exist anymore.
I want to see you open the door, walk into my room, and knell down to kiss me.
That's all I want in life.
I know I can't hold on to the night forever, but just one moment with you in my dream and that'd make me happy.
I want nothing else but to see you smile at me.
I want to feel your arms around me and want your love even though I know when I wake up you'll be gone.

Hold You In My Dreams

I want to hold you tenderly in my dreams.
Hold you and never let go even if it'll only last for one second or one brief moment in my dreams.
I'll hold you in my hands and never let go because once I do I'll wake up and everything will be over.
All hopes and happiness will once again die.
I want to hold the happiness as close as I can because each minute of happiness is each minute that I'll smile through the tears.
I can never forget your face or voice.
The many words you said and the sweet songs, they still echo but you're nowhere to be found.
All I can do is dream.
Dream of you, though, reality hurts when dreams die.
I wish I could dream forever and hold you in my heart.
Dream the night away because once the darkness disappears the sun will rise, and when I open my eyes, the bed will be empty without your love.
The happiness will die with your love.
I wish I could dream forever and make this life a false happiness even if it takes everything I have.
I would rather have you in my dreams than never to have you at all.

I Don't Want To Love

Love is a dream.
Our love was dream, and it'll always be for me.
I dream of the a peaceful and joyful love, but waking up only brings a sad and lonely dream.
I don't want to love, and don't want to know or feel the pain of loving someone.
I'm afraid of love, and afraid to love someone who either truly loves or hurts me.
Dreams are dreams because they're already too hurtful when I wake up.
How would my love be like when it's reality?
How would I be when my love decides to walk away?
How hurt would I be when my love decides to have another dream and leaves me behind in my lonely space?
I don't want to love because it'll only kill me softly while my heart bleeds uncontrollably.

I Love You

I love you...
I love you with all my heart.
Even in my dreams I'm in love with you.
I love you...
I love you with all the tears that I cry when you're not with me.
I cry when you're far away and we can't be together.
I love you with all my life.
I love you, but do you really know it?
Do you ever look at me?
I smile at you but you never seem to feel my love.
You never talk or speak a tender word of love when we're together.
What's in your heart and mind?
When will you tell me you love me?
How many seasons will we have to live when you finally look at me and tell me how much you love me?
How many days and nights will pass by before you express your feelings to me?
I can't live or love you forever.
My heart will die, my soul will disappear, and my hair will turn gray.
I can't wait forever to hear you say you love me.

In The Memory Of Love

One day in the distant future when you look back at our love just remember you were the one who said goodbye.
Remember that you were the one who missed the time and tears of happiness during those beautiful autumn afternoons.
One day when you walk down that lonely path, I hope you'll still remember my name.
Remember the kiss we had that I gave to you with all the dreams and heart.
I gave it all to you in that one kiss only hoping you'd love me in return.
I hope in your dreams there'll be a piece of our love left.
I hope the new kiss with your new love won't be the same kiss like ours.
I only hope you'll still love me the same way in our memory of love.
I wish you the best and wish you the happiness I'll never have.
While I walk alone on this empty street as the rain falls down, I'll remember you.
I'll remember each word you told me and, hopefully, I'll still feel a bit of your happiness beside me.

It's Everyone's Dream

Sometimes I want to tell you I love you, but when I'm alone with you I can't seem to open my mouth.
I just can't tell you what I've been feeling for a very long time.
Sometimes I want to hold and kiss you, but I can never do any of that.
It's everyone's dream to have someone like you.
If only you knew that I love you.
If only I know the way to tell you my deepest feelings.
I'm nervous and shy, but I know deep inside I love you.
Sometimes the way you talk makes me wonder about you.
The way you move makes me think of you night and day.
If only you knew that I love you.
It's everyone's dream to be close to you and it's anyone's fault to let you go.
I guess I'll have to keep it to myself the love I have for you.
I'll take you into my heart and keep the happy memories we have together.

Just Heartbreak

If I tell you I don't love you, will you understand?
If I tell you I have to go, will you be happy?
I want to be with you forever but time and destiny won't allow.
I want to hold you every second of the day and tell you I love you, but the words don't come out right.
Will you be sad if I never look you in your eyes like you want me to?
Will you be mad at me if the words that come out of my mouth aren't the words you want to hear?
I want to love you with every second of the day and wake up next to you, but it could never be what we wish for.
Every time you look at me it hurts my heart.
Every time I see you walk down the street I want to run to you and hold you, but whenever I try to do it I just lose my strength.
I want to scream out loud the words you want to hear me say.
I want to look into those tender eyes and kiss you, but whenever you stand before me the tender lips just can't touch one another.
I want to touch your hands and feel your warmth.
I want to walk down the sunset and live happily ever after, but our love story could never be a fairytale.
I can only dream of tomorrow and hope my dreams will last forever like you'll forever be in my heart.

Just One Lonely Dream

When I was young I thought love was a beautiful thing.
I thought love comes and goes like a dream.
I didn't realize how love really felt and didn't know how much it'd hurt when you fall in love.
I didn't know love was one lonely dream.
I looked into your eyes and it was like a dream when you smiled at me.
I loved those eyes and loved your voice when you called my name.
I drifted away like in a dream and you were always there to make sure I was happy.
I held you close and loved you every day of my life.
When the sun went down you were beside me and when the moon came up you were there singing me to sleep.
You were the one who kept me alive and were the one who showed me how love really should be.
But you were also the one who showed me the pain in love when you walked away leaving me to the night.
You were the one who left in those warm beautiful afternoons waiting for love to return.

Keep Our Dreams Alive

You're no longer in love with me.
I could see it in your eyes.
There aren't any looks of love in those eyes like the first time you looked at me the first day we met.
Nothing is there in your eyes now.
The kisses are no longer passionate enough while the tears fall deep inside my heart.
I hold you close, so close and tenderly, trying not to let go because once I do, it'd no longer be you and me.
You've walked away and no longer remember ofour dreams and all the passionate nights we shared.
I hold you tight to keep our dreams alive and keep the love lock inside my heart.
No matter what happens today and no matter what you say I'll always hold on to our love.
Maybe I'm too weak to let go, and too weak to watch you walk away.
Now the dreams are here, but you're no longer with my love.
You're no longer the bird that stands by my side during those nights of loneliness.

Kiss Goodbye

I knew there were others I could've loved, but with you I felt something different
With you, I felt like a flower growing in your love.
With you, I felt like a bird with the freedom to fly above the horizon.
I knew you'd never be the perfect lover.
I could sense you weren't the one who could keep the promises.
But somehow I couldn't let you go.
I couldn't stop loving you and didn't know why.
Whenever you talked to me I forgot about reality.
I put my love and heart into your world.
I fell deep down into that world without broken dreams and realistic promises.
When you held me tight that evening, I saw something special happening in our lives.
But the kiss you gave me wasn't what I thought because it was a kiss goodbye.
When you walked out the door I was dead.
You waved goodbye and the sky fell down on me.
I couldn't breathe or see anything.
The world ended and life was all but over.
I didn't know what I'd done because you didn't tell me when you kissed me goodbye.
I knew from that moment I'd live in misery trying to figure out why you'd walked away.
You gave me a passionate kiss on my lips but it wasn't what I thought.
A kiss that turned out to be a kiss of goodbye.
The kiss of love I'd remember forever, but would you?

Kiss Me Once Again

You gave me the first kiss on my lips.
It was the first kiss that'd be with me forever.
You gave me a dream I thought would last like the passing time.
The kiss that lingered vividly in my thoughts.
It was so dreamy and tenderly when when our lips touched.
You held me as if you didn't want to let go of my love.
The feeling and sensation were so good, but within a blink of the eyes you were gone from my life.
My life shattered when I lost your love with the darkness.
Everything fell apart when you went far away from this heart.
Kiss me once again to let me have the feeling of being loved by someone.
Your love were warm and sweet.
I want you back in my life like the good old times.
Come back and kiss me once again with your tender lips.

Let Me Forget My Youth

Let me forget my youth.
Let me forget that moment when you were still here and time wasn't passing by so quickly and suddenly.
Let me forget my youth.
Forget the time when love was young and we were happy together.
The dreams and hopes, everything was bright like the stars above the night sky.
The vivid images of us holding hands during those afternoon walks.
The laughter we gave to the room filled with memories.
Those were the happy days when I was so happy.
I could never forget them.
But then again, what was here before should be forgotten.
I must learn to let go because time is running out and dreams are fading fast.
There's nothing left between us but our memories.
The moments I had with you will be with me forever.
The kisses we had before you left I'll hold on in my heart.
Those nights together and those happy times will be with me until the end of time.
I hope you the best and hope you'll be happy with your new love.
I hope the best for you always.

Letting Go

They all told me to let go, but how could I?
If love was that easy to let in and out, would it really be love?
You were the bright and happy moment in my life.
The sun could rise and set, but you were always there for me.
When we broke up nothing in my life was the same.
I sat home all day waiting for the phone to ring.
When it finally did ring, I'd pick it up praying it'd be you, but it always was someone else.
I tried and told myself to let go of your image in my heart, but it was easier said than done.
When the shadow began creeping up in my room, I just pretend I'm hearing you laugh.
I turned around to laugh with you but all I saw was empty space.
When the lights went out I once again found the silence and darkness of the lonely night.
I slept days and nights away because they helped me forget about those times with you.
I was finally able to let you out of my heart.
I had no dream, saw nothing and heard no voice.
Things were normal all over again.
Yet, once the sun rose above the horizon and I woke up from my sleep, it once again hit me that you'd left.
I once again found that letting go of you would take a very long time.

Lonely Heart

With all the promises you gave me, you turned away and left me.
All the words of love were only lies because you never really meant what you said about staying with me forever.
You walked away without saying a word.
If only you could've stayed for a moment to make me happy.
Why must you leave my lonely heart?
All the dreams now lie on the ground broken to pieces.
Where do I start?
Where do I go to find your love again?
Where have you gone to?
What will tomorrow be like when we meet again?
Will you look at me and smile, or will you walk off and not say a word?
What will your heart be?
Where will your mind be knowing I still love you?
I'll smile at the pain knowing you'll never return.
What more could I do but lie in bed and listen to the falling rain?
Listen to the footsteps that'll never come back.
Think and dream as though you've never walked away.
All the dreams will last forever, but all and all, they'll never come true without you in my life.

Love Is Not Meant To Stay

When love goes, it goes far away leaving you empty.
It flies away and leaving you to beg for another chance.
Love dies and time stops still as you hurt over and over.
We live forever forgetting and forgiving each other for the lost of time.
We saw in our dreams the direction our love was going so why fight a battle that we can't win?
Why ask to stay?
Why not let go when you don't love me anymore?
Let go of all the pain we left on each other.
Let go rather than to think about it day and night.
Don't hold on and wonder about something that no longer exists in our lives.
Why think about something you can never hold on to again in your lifetime?
If love is not meant to stay then we should let it go.
If love is not meant to stay then let it go into the thing air.
Love is no more between us.
If there isn't a chance to change our lives then don't fight or beg for love to stay.

Me And The Night

Should I be mad at you?
Should I cry during the lonely nights?
What should I do?
I've searched for love and the special arms that'd hold me when I feel lonely.
Now that I've found you I wonder if you also love me too?
Maybe I'm daydreaming.
Maybe the love between us is only me thinking about you at night and dreaming about you during the day.
I don't want to lie to myself or my heart because I do love you.
I walk to your house and you're not there.
I can't find you anywhere and I don't know what to do.
I call you but you don't answer, and when you do, you're always telling me you're busy.
I don't know what to say anymore.
I can't let you go, but what should I do?
I tell myself not to see you but I always end up looking for you.
Your love has captured my heart deeply.
Even though I don't know if it's true love or not, it's too good to let go.
At this moment, I'm here with the lonely night.
It's me and the darkness thinking of you.
I don't know what to do but to sit and wait for your call.

Me Or You (300th Poem)

Who is it to blame, me or you, for the mistakes in our lives?
Who's to blame when the music dies and we stop dancing while I cry about tomorrow?
Where would I go?
Where would I be without you?
Me or you, who's to blame when tomorrow dies and we look back at yesterday knowing our love was so wonderful?
Why did it have to end so badly?
Why had there been so many tears falling in our love when there was nothing that could've broken us up?
I can't dream or think anymore.
Even the world has stopped turning because our love has ended.
I can't believe the dreams we've had together now have turned into a world of nightmares.
Can you dream again with me?
Can you live without my love?
I can't live or dream anymore without you.
I can't see the daylight even though the sun is shining.
I can't see the stars even though the moon is bright above the dreamful night sky.

Moonlight Without You

I still remember when we stood under the moonlight and dreamed the night away.
I used to think you were the one as we lay in bed in those cold nights.
Under the moonlight I dreamed of you.
Today, I don't know what to dream about anymore.
The moonlight still shines brightly while my heart bleeds for your love.
I stand here beneath the moonlight trying to figure out what went wrong in our relationship.
I want to go back to those days and change the things that killed our love.
I want to change those moments when we hurt each other.
I want to be able to hold you again before I close my eyes under the moonlight and fall into my deepest dream.
I watch the moonlight without you because you've walked away.
You went slowly while I stood under the moonlight and watched as your footsteps fadedaway.
I let you go without stopping you, but if you'd cared at all then you'd have stayed.
My heart now fears the loneliness of tomorrow, but do you care?
Do you know what I'm going through?

Heartbreak Love Poems by NGHI NGUYEN

Never Fall In Love Again

When we first met you said there was only the two of us in this world.
You said in this world our love was the greatest and there was no one else who you'll love but me.
You said my love was like the air you breathed.
But now those words have vanished with the air.
They've faded into the darkness like a night that passes by into the morning light.
Your words are gone and I'll never hear them again.
I'll never be able to touch your hands and walk with you into the evening.
I'll never fall in love again with anyone else, these were the words you said when you held me close and kissed me.
You were the world to me because when you were there, every step in my life were magnificent.
Every day that I lived were beautiful with the sun walking with me as I heard your laughter.
But you were only give me those dreams and lies to make me happy.
After the light faded you waved goodbye and I died slowly without you.
I know from now on I'll never fall in love again with someone who tells me sweet words.
I'll never love someone who promises to be with me forever because it'd only last from the very beginning.
This love will never walk with me until the very end.
I'll never fall love again knowing from my past that love can hurt much more when you take those promises in and they turn into lies.

Never Look Back To Yesterday

It's too late now for us to go back and love each other like when love first blossomed in our lives.
Don't waste a tear, and don't cry because we both know we can't have those happy memories again.
We'd shared many memories, breathed the air, and listened to our beating hearts together.
We were living in a world where happy times lived forever without sadness.
Now that we're apart, what else is here for us but heartbreak?
There's nothing to hold on but heartache.
Never look back to yesterday and smile or cry because in our hearts and minds we were never with each other even though we said we were.
Never look back to yesterday and tell yourself why we ended up like this.
We knew this was coming right at the very moment when we kissed and that kiss wasn't what we both wanted.
If we were to meet again, what should we say?
What would you tell me?
What would I tell you?
What will our hearts be then?
Will we be happy like when we first met?
We'll never know until that very moment comes and hits us like a dream.

Night Falls

Night has fallen as memories flash by like a river of dreams.
I remember many loving memories but the one I love now is like an ocean's current.
The waves have come in and gone out, never to come back.
Many nights I've waited and many nights I've dreamed but I just can't get you out of my mind.
There're many things I want to tell you and many words I have to say but I can't seem to do either when we're together.
Now I wait for you but don't know why.
I wait when my heart is dead and my dreams have all died on that beautiful day when you walked away.
I have no more dreams because they've all turned into nightmares.
I want to say I'm sorry and that I love you, but whenever I see you the words get stuck in my throat.
I know I've left you pain, but there're many words I have to tell you to forget and forgive all the pain.
I love you but it's just that I can't say it.
If we could go back, I wish you'd never known me.
I wish I'd never loved you.
Loving you was the greatest thing in my life, but then again, loving you was also the greatest pain in my life.

Once We Are Apart

The love poems you've written and the love you've shared with me, I'll cherish everything.
I'll keep them like my dreams and wishes that I've always wanted to come true.
I know you really love me but also know you're in love with someone else.
I know the love poems aren't just for me but also someone else.
Still, I love and forgive you.
I'll forgive the pain you've created.
I know your heart belongs to someone else.
Yet, I'll never get mad at you or be sad once we're apart.
The love that's here will stay with me.
I know my dreams mean nothing now, but I'll hold on to them.
I know you'll love me forever and I'll never hate you for loving someone else.
You know you've hurt me badly and I forgive you because love hurts.
The truth of what's happening is only pain.
The pain you've caused me and the love you've given me will stay.
What we have I'll forever cherish, and forever, I'll remember you.

One Dream Of You

Last night I dreamed of you.
I dreamed you came home and smiled at me.
You took me into your arms and kissed me.
The dream was so real I thought it was really happening and that you were really there with me.
I thought it'd last forever but when the telephone rang you were gone.
The dream was gone but it made me so happy thinking about it.
I was floating under the sky of dreams.
The dream took me to a place where I could be with you.
It was like that secret place when we were together.
I remember that moment when I held you tight, yet, I had to let go.
I couldn't hold on when you were tired of me.
I couldn't dream forever when your love grew old and you wanted to go.
One dream of you and I forgot about reality.
You aren't coming back and you'd never will.
You've gotten what you wanted and needed.
While I'm here dreaming about us, you're somewhere else dreaming about life and someone new.
If reality hurts then I'd rather close my eyes and dream about you.
I'll dream the night away to be with only you.
I'll dream of love and dream of something in life that'll never happen.

One Heart, One Love

There's only one heart and one love.
I have one heart and I give it to you.
I have one love and it belongs to you.
What more can I give to let you know I truly love you?
I knew from the beginning I'd put myself into your arms.
I knew when I spent more time with you I'd fall in love, and when I loved you too much, I'd never be able to let go.
Today, I've loved you with all my heart.
I can't barely relax or eat without thinking about you.
In the night I can't even close my eyes and fall asleep without thinking about what you're doing at your house.
When I dream, I dream of you.
I dream about us being together, and you'd love me with one heart and one love.
When I wake up the first thing that comes to mind is whether or not you're thinking about me.
Everyday is the same and everyday is all about you.
Nothing can take my mind away from you.
You're all I think about, but you're never there.
You never call and never say you love me.

Only In My Dream

The first time I saw you I knew I was in love and you were the one.
The way you talked and looked at me, I was sure you were the one.
I thought about you night and day.
I couldn't close my eyes once without seeing you.
I thought of you every second, minute, and hour.
You were the one for me but I couldn't express my thoughts.
All day and night, there was nothing but you in my head.
Still, I couldn't tell you I loved you.
Only in my dream could I tell you.
Only in my dream could I hold you.
My dreams allowed me to kiss your gentle lips.
My dreams gave me your love.
There were many ways I could've expressed myself to you, but I couldn't seem to find one.
I wanted to be close to you, but how could I when I couldn't bring myself to express my love to you?
If I could only see you in my dreams to tell you I really loved you.
Only in my dreams could I hold you forever.

Our Love Lives Forever

I hear your voice vividly but I can't find your love.
With all my heart I've devoted myself to you yet you never love me.
I hear your voice like I've never before, the voice that took away my sadness.
With all my love I'll wait and love you for the rest of my life.
But right now, you've gone forever from my life.
I need you with me, with my heart and my love.
Do you still love me?
Yesterday is gone and our dreams are gone with it.
I think of you, and with all the dreams, I'll wait.
Your love will keep me awake.
Can you hear me cry?
The love I've given you will never die like the sun above.
My love will never go and leave you alone.
I want to be with you so come and hold me tight.
Stay here with me.
Come and never let go of my hands because your love will always make me happy.
With all my dreams I'll wait.
With all my love, my heart, and our memories I'll wait forever.

Dream ~ Living Out Of Reality

Please Don't Be Sad

Please don't be sad when we've fallen apart.
I'll never forget all the lovely times we'd spent together.
I'll never forget the first kiss I'd given you.
I know you'll forget all the love songs we've shared and all the love I've given you.
I'll be the one who remembers while you'll forget the first kiss you gave me.
I'll be the one who remembers of those tender moments.
I won't be mad at the pain in our love.
I'll forget everything you've done because they were the lies of yesterday romance.
I know you'll forget the words and melodies in our love songs.
You'll forget that one moment when you told me I was the one you loved.
You'll forget everything that was once so beautiful to each other.
I'll not hate you.
Instead, I'll remember and forgive.
I'll forgive you because when we were together everything was just a dream.
So please don't be sad because our love was never really living in reality.

Please Give Me One Last Moment

Please, please give me one last moment to regret, to think and dream of those happy days with you.
Please, please give me one last moment to remember of my youth.
Remember when time was with me, when flowers grew outside my windows and life was happier than ever.
The loneliness and emptiness surround me when I'm without you.
All the wines now taste like my falling tears.
Drink, that's all I can do to forget today and the last moment I was with you.
Please give me one last moment, that's all I need now.
Let me be with you for one moment before I close my eyes and fall asleep to leave this world and all the memories behind.
The pain took over my life the day you said goodbye.
Then the clouds covered the sky and darkness filled my heart.
The sorrows of seeing you walked away have killed me ever since.
Please, please give me one last moment, one last kiss before I close my eyes and sleep.
Please, please give me one last moment for me to regret, for me to think and dream of those happy days with you.

Quickly, You Are Gone

One minute you're with me and the next I don't know where you are.
One minute the word love is close and the next the word love seems to tear me apart.
The word love coming from your mouth is like thunder on a stormy day, and you're the storm in my life.
One moment we laugh and the next we're done.
You're laughing in your new life while I'm crying in mine.
I'm still living in our dreams while in your heart our dreams have died.
They no longer belong to us, but instead belong to you and your new love.
Quickly, you're gone out of my heart.
Why are there so many loves and heartbreaks when you come and go, and all that's left are tears and laughter?
You're gone and no one can stop you or change your mind.
You're the wind and the needles that wound my heart and my soul.
You don't know and don't care that I'm hurting.
You walked away; you just walked away from me.

Rain, Wash Away My Sorrows

How many days have passed since we walked together on this road?
How many dreams have died since the very last moment I held you in my arms?
What's there to feel when the rain comes?
What's there to remember with that kiss when dreams are washed away with the rain?
How many times has it rain when I'm here in bed without you?
How many raindrops will it take for me to count before I finally accept the truth that you're gone?
There are so many lies and rainy days in love.
But where am I to go?
What am I suppose to do under the gray sky when you're not here?
Rain, wash away my sorrows and pain.
Rain, wash away the tears that are tearing up my heart.
Tomorrow or today, they're all the same when I'm without you.
No love in the rain and no tears in the night.
There's only heartbreak thinking about you.
There's only heartache in all the memories we've shared.

Remaining Dreams of Love

No dream lasts forever.
If we could go back and relive our dreams, what would be different this time around?
If I could go back I don't want to give you all of my heart knowing you'd never do the same.
My dreams of yesterday are now gone.
Only in my sleep can I touch your face and kiss those lips.
Only in my dreams can I see your eyes looking at me.
But dreams can't last forever can they?
They can only go as far as the darkness of the night allows them to be.
When the sun rises over the distance the smile will fade and the feeling of love will turn back to sadness.
If I could dream forever I'd dream of you.
If I could live forever I'd love you.
But no dream continues forever through the daylight.
No one lives forever.
Just like what our love has shown, dreams can only last for a brief moment.

Requests

I hold to my heart the happiness that's in me.
I hold on to your hands trying not to let go because you're all I have and ever wanted.
You're all I've ever needed.
Why must you leave?
Why must love be so cruel and unkind to me?
What have I done to deserve this?
Can I have one more day and one more kiss?
Can I have one more look at your face?
Why must I always be the one who gets left behind?
Why must I always be the one who loses in love?
I was happy when I found you because I couldn't dream of something better in life.
You came to me like a dream and I loved you so much.
Now this dream turns into a nightmare.
In a blink of an eye you walked off and left me wondering what life would be like when the sun rises tomorrow.
When the years go by, who'll be here to comfort me?
In the hard times that I'll face and in the days when my hair turns gray, who'll be here?
I don't have you anymore and never will be again.

River Of Love

Eyes to eyes, I gave my love to you.
Through the happiness and sadness there was always your love lifting me up.
The smile on your face and those beautiful eyes made life so much easier for me.
We loved each other like no others had ever before.
Hand in hand, we walked while we thought about tomorrow.
It was going to be the two of us forever.
Nevertheless, I couldn't help but ask how long love was going to last?
How long would you be staying with me?
There were so many questions, but I tried to not think too much about them.
I lived a happy life with you and you were the very happiness I needed to survive.
But things fell apart when you decided to end our love one winter day.
Your love was the river that frozen solid.
The river of love that once gave me dreams and hopes stopped moving with the winter wind.
I watched you go like watching the river dry up before my eyes.

Same Time, Same Place

I lay you down and this is the last time we'll ever see each other.
This will be our final moment face to face and eyes to eyes.
These tears I cry for you and forever I don't know who I'll be crying for.
I don't know who I'll love like the way I've loved you.
There're so many questions I need answers too.
I don't know who to turn to and don't know what to say when people talk to me.
There won't be any more words to speak when I open my mouth knowing the person next to me from now on won't be you.
All the love and dreams won't be the same without you.
Maybe in another time and place we'll meet again with the same dreams and love.
We'll once again be happy like before.
It'll be like the first time we met when we shared our love.
We can relive the first kiss and all other memories when we meet again in that wonderful happy place.

Searching For Love

The first time I learned to love I found a person whom I thought I'd spend my life with.
The months went by and I lived in happiness.
The laughter built up, but it all ended when love ended.
She walked away from it all and my heart fell apart.
One perfect dream shattered as the warmth and caring comfort died with the cold winter.
I stood alone trying to cope with the situation.
I never cried even through the pain she'd inflicted on me.
I never fell in love again fearing the same thing would happen again.
I searched for love and found it, but it didn't last.
I went searching for love, but love never stayed with my heart.
I thought about her more and more while spending the nights alone.
I wanted to share my feelings with someone but there was none.
My love was like the wind that came and went.
I tried to grab hold of her but she passed right through me.
Today, I'm still searching for love.
I search for the one who'd love me even though I still fear love.
I don't know when or where, but I hope this person will come soon.

Sing For The Lonely One

One day you came and said you loved me.
My heart was pounding so fast when you told me you wanted me to be the one in your life.
Like a beautiful dream that came true, your love were the greatest happiness I cared for.
One day you came under a beautiful blue sky and sang the love songs.
You memorized the words to celebrate our love.
You sang to make me smile with your voice so sweet.
It was the greatest voice I'd ever heard and the only voice I'd kept in my heart.
Then one day I woke up to see the rain falling outside my windows and beside my bed there was no one.
You were gone and all I got was a letter.
I couldn't believe what was happening.
Nothing was left but a heart that was broken in pieces.
I sat there waiting for you as the songs played with all the memories you'd left behind in our love.
Each lovely word erased the pain and memories in my heart.
I could do nothing but wait for your love.

Sing For The Lonely World

If I sing, would the world sing with me?
Sing the sad love songs and sing the words that'd break my heart.
Would anyone drink with me?
Drink to forget the lonely world and sing to forget life really exists.
Let the lyrics to a sad love song be my life.
I want to hum the melodies slowly like the tears falling down my face.
How much can I forget with this wine?
How many memories of you can I throw away?
When the wine fades away, I'll sit and listen to the sad love songs all over again.
I'd make believe the songs are written for me and I'll sing in my own sedation.
I'll close my eyes and fantasize a beautiful dream of you, or would it be a nightmare?
The kiss and love, how painful it'll be to feel them again and to relive those sorrows and pains you've left.
What will I sing?
Maybe I'll just sing for the lonely world full of sadness.

Sing For The One Yesterday

I knew loving you was only a pain in my life.
I tried to tell myself if you were to leave one day, it'd mean nothing.
I thought everything would be normal, but now I realize I love you too much.
How could I lie to myself and pretend you were just one of the many who I've loved and let go?
You were different and you meant more to me than anyone else ever did.
Everything has fallen apart today with the laughter gone.
The sweet loving kisses have vanished like your love.
Everything is gone like the memories of the sweet melodies you'd sung to me.
They're now the clouds moving back and forth waiting to dissolve away into thin air like your love.
How could I've been so foolish to think I could forget you easily when deep down I loved you so much?
I could never forget you or fight against the truth that your love was stronger than my will.
What can I say now that you're gone?
It's too late to tell you anything.
It's too late to hold on to you when the distance has grown apart.
I love you forever and will never forget you.

Sorry Does Not Work

I'm tired of hearing you say you're sorry.
I'm tired of seeing the lights go out and you're not with me.
You're not in bed and I have no idea where you are.
There are days when you're not here.
I can't explain what you're thinking anymore.
Is love dying on us?
There's nothing more heartbreaking than to sit here thinking about love while you're thinking about something else on your mind.
Is there still love between us?
Do you think of me or someone else when you're alone?
Sorry doesn't work, it just doesn't work anymore.
I can't live with you while you're living in dreams.
I feel I'm the only one who tries hard to keep our love together while you're thinking about leaving.
Sorry doesn't work when you say it so many times but never mean it.
What do we have to do?
What do I have to do to keep your love in one place?
What do I have to say to find out if you truly love me ?
What do I need to do to give our love a better future?

That Day Without You

If the wind could talk, would it tell me lies?
Would it tell me 'I love you'?
Those were the three words you constantly told me when I thought you really did love me.
Through all the lies and tears you'd given me, why did I still love you so much?
Why did I still hope to see you again?
Maybe through all those lies there was happiness that only you could've given me even from the tears to the pain of knowing you never really loved me.
In my heart the lies were all I had with and without you.
Once in love even all the lies could be true.
Even the heartbreak and the tears could be turned into happiness.
My dream of being together forever faded with the slamming of the door.
I could go on and pick up where you'd left off but forever and ever I could only love you.
I'd always love and have you in my heart, even if every word you told me were lies.

The End

Why won't you tell me what's inside your mind?
Why won't you tell me what you're thinking in your heart?
I can't ask you what's in your heart because I want you to tell me whatever you're feeling.
Don't make me beg.
I love you, but do you love me?
Do you ever think of me when you're walking alone on the road or driving in those lonely nights?
Do you think of me when you're in bed?
Who do you dream of at night?
Is it me or someone else?
What exactly are you feeling?
The end, it's the end of our love.
I know you don't love me, but for some reasons I can't stop loving you.
I'm in too deep because I love you and know I'm a fool.
I know I can find others who are better than you, but I don't want to let you go.
You don't love me and I can't beg you to.
No matter what I say or how much tears I give, you won't love me the way I love you.
You never think of me, so what do you want from me?
What do you want with this heart?

The Last Kiss Goodbye

I'm sitting here thinking of someone I'll be dreaming of tonight.
The last kiss or the last word goodbye then everything is over.
The time, day, memories, and the love we had now are in history like a passing wind.
I still remember the first time we were together.
I could never forget that special moment.
Everything we had was the greatest part of my life.
How could I ever forget them?
The last kiss goodbye will be the hardest, but will be the greatest in my love.
I want you to know all the love we had will stay alive with me.
I'll hold on to everything you've given me to this point.
I'll cherish all the love we had and all the joy you brought.
Every moment we've had forever will stay with me.

Tomorrow When Love Comes

I know dreams don't last forever, and also know many things in life aren't what I want them to be.
Happiness doesn't remain the same and dreams dissolve away when the night comes to an end.
At least in love I know I've been with you and will always cherish those moments.
I know tears don't fall without love, sadness, and heartbreak.
All the laughter doesn't come and go, but at least with you I know what tomorrow brings.
I cry today for happiness, but maybe I'll cry tomorrow when I lose you.
No matter what happens in life, I hope when tomorrow comes I'll still be with you.
I hope when love comes you'll be the one and your lips will be those I kiss.
I hope you'll be the shoulder I lean on when time is tough.
When winter comes I hope you'll be sitting next to me and you'll sing to warm my soul.
In the coldness of the night I hope you'll smile and let me slip away into dreams like all loneliness has never existed in my life.

Too Late To Hold On

Our love was a dream to me.
It was the sweetest dream I wanted to have and I wish it could've lasted longer.
I watched you go like the wind that blew across my face.
I watched you go as the rain fell down hard.
Each drop of rain reflected a memory we shared.
Looking back, those days together were perfect.
Nothing was standing in our way of love and all the sad things were pushed aside.
Life went by quickly and before I could open my eyes you were gone.
It was too late to hold on to what was then.
It was too late to tell you how much I loved you when you didn't care to hear.
Too late to bring back those happy years and relive each one in harmony.
I couldn't say much when you walked away.
I stood there and watched the smile faded away as you let go of my hands.
These hands still very much need you and your love in the cold and lonely nights to come.

Until The End

There's so much love in this world but there're also worries and emptiness.
As the lights go out and the night comes, love is not here or is it anywhere around me.
It's so quiet that sometimes I feel love has abandoned me.
Until the end, there's no love at all.
I search everywhere to find the perfect love, but there seems to be no perfect love in my life.
How many dreams have I had about love?
There's never a moment when I don't think about that one person who'd come and take my breath away.
Dreams will always be lovely dreams.
When I wake up I'll be alone in my empty bed.
Sometimes the loneliness creeps up and the pain hits me softly.
I hate my dreams and lonely life.
I have no love, pain, or tears; there's nothing here at all.
I know there'll be pain in love but just to love once, I'll sacrifice the pain to be able to hold and feel the warmth of that special someone.
I risk my heart to learn and feel love in my life for just one breathtaking moment.

When Our Love Did Go Wrong

When things started to go wrong with us I knew the end was near.
Our love was like the end of the love song that you used to play for me every night before we closed our eyes and fell asleep.
In my dream I saw us standing before the ocean watching the waves come in.
You'd sing to me and I'd fall into your arms and into your love.
Yet, when I woke up you weren't there.
I was alone in bed and there was no voice beside me singing that love song.
The word heartbreak never really hit me until the moment you said goodbye.
When the rain fell down on my shoulders it was the beginning of my tears when our love did go wrong.
The snow followed and the warmth wasn't with me anymore.
The hands and arms that once held me so tightly during those winter days were gone.

Words Of Pray

The special moments when you come and smiled at me.
The happy feeling when you kiss me goodbye, I wish I could have them one more time.
Days of waiting in my own solitude, but still, there's no sign of you.
My life is nothing but a rainy day waiting for you.
You're the sun in my life that comes out from behind the clouds.
I see your face in my dreams at night.
You smile at me as I open the door, but just right before I could hold you, the dreams end.
I think about you every minute as I pray for your love with words from the heart.
I pray one day you'll have a change of heart and return to me, but this is probably too much to hope for.
Like all my dreams, you'll probably never come.
I'm here watching the rain and hope it'll go away soon so when the sun comes out you'll be the face smiling down at me.

Wrong One To Kiss

The dream is over, but why am I still thinking about you?
Why is my heart so wounded when I know you've never loved me?
I was the one holding on to the hope that our love would blossom into something better.
Meanwhile, you didn't want anything to do with our love.
My heart wants to stop beating to forget about the pain, but my head feels differently.
I want to be like the wind that flows and flows, and never experience pain or sadness.
I want to fly away to forget this hurt you've left behind.
I want to forget the kiss and your face.
You were the wrong one to kiss on that beautiful spring day when our love story began.
Now I sit and count the many things I'd foreseen for our future.
The voice, eyes, and kisses you've left behind are too hard to forget.
I can't stop thinking about you even though I really want to.
There's nothing I can do and there're no words to express the hurt I feel inside.
You were the wrong one to kiss from the beginning and I wish I could take it all back.

Yesterday, Today, Tomorrow

When we took those vows I took every word into my heart.
From that moment on you were the one who I'd promised to love until the day I close my eyes.
I told you no matter what happens tomorrow you'd always be the one and only one.
I still keep those words even though you're no longer here.
I hope wherever you are that you never forget about me.
Remember the last time when we held hands and remember the first kiss we shared.
Sometimes I want to close my eyes and follow you to wherever you are, but I can't.
I may dream and wish, but we probably will never be together like the clouds and the sky.
The mornings will go by and the nights will die, but my love remains yours.
Seasons will come and go, but I won't forget even through the loneliest moment of my life.
I'll dream of you when Christmas comes and the snow falls outside.
I've loved you yesterday and I'll continue loving you today and tomorrow.
Yesterday, today, and tomorrow, my love will be the same even when my hair grays out.
I'll love you even more as each minute passes by knowing we'll meet when the time is right.

Yesterday Was A Dream

Yesterday, when you came to me you brought with you the smile that brightened up my life.
You were like a flower growing in my heart.
Yesterday, my dreams became reality when I met you.
The grass was green and the birds sang with spring, and it was all for me.
Today, I look back and wonder if reality came too quickly.
Maybe I was still living in my dreams and never woke up.
Perhaps it was really a nightmare instead of a beautiful dream as you walked away and the flowers withered in your footsteps.
The first time we held hands you'd kissed me on my lips.
I remember that sensational moment and still see the sparkle in your eyes.
No, they weren't dreams, every one of those moments with you.
It's just that they're the nightmares of today.
I need your love in the night when my loneliness takes over in this room.
All space and time seem to freeze up waiting for you.
I need your arms when I walk home alone and hear laughter in the distance while feeling lonely.
Yesterday, it's what I want right now.
Yesterday was love and dream, but it was something I had.
Today, the love is gone and the nightmare lingers around.
What am I suppose to do now?
What am I to do about yesterday?

You'll Always Be The One

In love there're no promise that we'll stay together forever.
I don't want to make promises with you then break them and cause you pain.
I don't want to give you too many hopes only to walk away and break your heart.
In love there's no guarantee we'll be together until our hair turn gray.
There won't be a road we can walk on forever.
There isn't a sunny sky that'll be above our heads forever.
In love there's no happiness that'll last forever, but there's one thing that exists in our love and that's eternity.
I won't make small or big promises to you but instead only to myself because I know I love you and will forever do.
I'll hold you in my heart, and only hope you'll do the same.
I don't want to hear you say you love me or hear about the promises you have for us.
If you really love me then you should always do so.
Don't tell me what we'll be doing tomorrow or that you'll be here with me forever.
Show me the future by being there when my hair turns gray.
Be there and hold my hands when the years pass by and I can no longer see the world as I did before or hear the sounds as softly as before.
Don't tell me tomorrow will be you and me.
Show me by being there when tomorrow comes.
If you really love me the future will tell me.
I don't need you to tell me with your words and I won't tell you what's in my heart.
I'll show you my love by being here with you until your last breath, and I can only pray you'll do the same.

Zoom My Heart Out

How big does my heart need to be to let you know I truly loved you?
I love you for who you are because you're always there when I need you.
You care for me like no others through your warmth and passion.
Do you know my heart belongs to you and only you?
Zoom my heart out to see the blood floating from your love.
Zoom my heart out to let you see what you mean to me.
I need you, but sometimes I don't think you know that.
You never understand my love for you or how important it is for me to have you in my life.
Our love is still tender and will always be the same forever.
No matter where the days take us, we'll always come back to these memories.
I know I'll always remember and love you.
I know I'll always taste the pain of loneliness whenever I think about you if you're not with me.

The End

INDEX

A

A Fool For You, **11**
A Fool In Love, **161**
A Song For Our Love, **162**
Acceptance of Love, **12**
Afternoon Of Love, **163**
Age Seventeen, **13**
All Out Of Tears, **14**
All That's Left, **164**
All The Nights Waiting, **15**
Alone Again With Love, **16**
Alone, **16**
Always The Last To Know, **17**
Another Day, **17**
Another Sad Goodbye, **18**
Another Try, **18**

B

Baby Try, **19**
Back To You, **19**
Be A Man, **20**
Because There Was You, **20**
Before The Goodbye, **21**
Before The Sad Goodbye, **23**
Before The Night Takes You Away, **22**
Before You Say Goodbye, **164**
Breath Of Love, **165**
Breathing For You, **24**
Bring Those Days Back To Me, **25**
Broken Dreams, **26**
Broken Heart Never Sleeps, **27**
By The Passing Hours, **28**
Bye, Bye, Baby, **29**

C

Can't See A Broken Heart, **29**
Close To My Heart, **30**
Closer In Time, **31**
Cold Nights, **165**
Cold Touch, **32**
Come To Me, **33**
Come Close To Me, **32**
Courage To Say Goodbye, **33**
Crazy About You, **34**
Cry For Our Love, **34**
Crying Is Just More Pain, **166**
Crying Shoulder, **167**
Curtain Close, **35**

D

Daydreaming, **168**
Days Of Loneliness, **36**
Deeply In Love, **37**

Did You See It Breaking?, **38**
Distance Between Us, **39**
Don't Cry For Our Love, **39**
Don't Forget Me, **40**
Don't Know What To Say, **40**
Don't Leave Me, **199**
Don't Let Go Of Time, **41**
Don't Let The Sun Go up, **42**
Don't Say Goodbye, **43**
Don't Say You Love Me, **199**
Dreaming For What?, **200**
Dreams Gone Out Of Our Hands, **201**
Dying Dreams, **201**
Dying Love, **44**

E

Ease My Sorrows, **45**
Easy To Say Goodbye, **46**
Emptiness, **47**
Enough Pain In Loving You, **47**
Even Good Dreams Fly, **202**
Even The Birds Sang, **169**
Everything Is Forgiven, **202**
Eyes Of Pain, **203**

F

Faded Love, **48**
Fading Footsteps, **49**
Falling In Love, **50**
Final Goodbye, **51**
For The One Who Said Goodbye, **170**
For You I Write, **170**
Forever Gone, **52**
Forever Is A Word, **203**
Forever Waiting, **53**
Forgetful, **54**
Forget Love, **204**
Forgetting Is Remembering, **171**
Forget Those Dreams, **204**

G

Gentle Heart, **205**
Gently, You Held Me Close, **206**
Give Me One More Chance, **171**
Gone With Happiness, **207**
Goodbye To Yesterday, **55**
Goodbye To You, **56**
Goodnight To Love, **57**
Got To Hold On, **172**

H

Happiness Gone By, **58**

Happiness Through Tonight, 59
Hate Or Love, 60
Have I Found The Right One?, 207
Have You Really Walked Away?, 60
Heart Of Pain, 61
Heartbreak, 61
Heartbreakingly, 62
Heartbroken, 173
Hearts Beating, 174
Heaven Is Lost, 62
Hello, Goodbye, 63
Hold Me One Last Time, 64
Hold On To Tonight, 208
Hold You In My Dreams, 209
How Could I Have Known?, 65

I

I Accept, 65
I Didn't Mean It At All, 66
I Don't Want To Fade Away, 67
I Don't Want To Love, 210
I Have Lost You, 68
I Have No One Left, 68
I Love You, 210
I Said I Love You, 69
I Wanted To Be Love, 70
If Only, 71
If There Was Another Chance, 72
If You Knew, 73
If You Want To Say I Love You, 73
In Love, 74
In The Distance, 74
In The Memory Of Love, 211
In The Nights, 75
It's Everyone's Dream, 212

J

July 4th, 2
Just Heartbreak, 3
Just One Lonely Dream, 3
Just One Wish, 2
Just To Know You're There, 2
Just To Love And Die, 2
Just You In My Heart, 2

K

Keep Our Dreams Alive, 214
Kindness Within You, 29
Kiss Goodbye, 215
Kiss Me Before You Say Goodbye, 79
Kiss Me Once Again, 216
Kisses On My Lips, 80
Knowing To Love Is To Die, 80

L

Last Day, 81
Late Love, 82

Laughing From The Heartbreak, 83
Let Me Forget My Youth, 216
Letting Go, 217
Lonely Heart, 218
Lonely, I Sing, 175
Lonely Street, 84
Losing Love, 176
Love Has Come And Gone, 84
Love Has Faded Away, 176
Love In My Heart (400th Poem), 177
Love In No Means, 177
Love Is Not Meant To Stay, 219
Love Just Had To Die On Me, 85
Love Me, Love You, 86
Love You For Ten Thousand Years, 86
Love, 87
Loving You Hurt So Much, 88
Loving You With All My Heart, 89
Lying To Myself, 89

M

Me And The Night, 219
Me Or You, 220
Midnight Without Love, 90
Moments Of Mistakes, 91
Moments of Truth, 92
Moonlight Without You, 221
Music In The Night, 178
My Loneliness With You, 92
My Love, If Only You Knew, 93
My Love Is True, 94
My Memories of Yesterday, 179
My Tears Are Burning Red, 95

N

Never Fall In Love Again, 222
Never Look Back To Yesterday, 223
Never Should I Cry, 180
Night Falls, 224
Nights Of Loneliness, 96
No One To Wait, 97
No Way Back, 98
Nothing Here But Tears, 99
Nothing Left But Memories, 100

O

Once We Are Apart, 225
Once You Are Gone, 181
One Day, 103
One Day In Love, 101
One Day Much Closer, 102
One Dream Of You, 226
One Heart, One Love, 227
One Last Tear For Tomorrow, 104
One Love Story, 105
One Night Of Passion, 106
One Silent Night, 107
Only In My Dream, 228

Our Love Lives Forever, **228**
Our Love Songs, **182**
Our Time Was Up, **108**
Over The Heartbreak, **109**

P

Pain You Give Me, **110**
Passing Time, **111**
Pieces of Me, **112**
Play The Song, **182**
Please Don't Be Sad, **229**
Please Forget The Days Gone By, **113**
Please Give Me One Last Moment, **229**
Prayer For Our Love, **114**
Prisoner Of Your Love, **115**
Promises To Keep, **116**

Q

Quickly, The Days Will Pass, **117**
Quickly, You Are Gone, **230**
Quietness, **183**

R

Rain, Wash Away My Sorrow, **230**
Remaining Dreams of Love, **231**
Requests, **231**
Right Here Waiting, **183**
River Of Lost, **118**
River Of Love, **232**
Road Of Love, **119**
Road To Nowhere, **120**
Run, **184**

S

Sad About Love, **121**
Sad With Love, **184**
Sad, **123**
Sad Memories, **122**
Same Time, Same Place, **233**
Searching For Love, **234**
Shadow Of The Night, **124**
Silent Music, **185**
Sing For The Lonely Hearts, **185**
Sing For The Lonely One, **234**
Sing For The Lonely World, **235**
Sing For The Lying Tears, **186**
Sing For The One In My Heart, **186**
Sing For The One Yesterday, **235**
Sing To Yesterday Love, **125**
Smile To Hide The Pain, **126**
Sometimes, **127**
Song For The Dead, **187**
Sorry Does Not Work, **236**

Stop The Days From Passing By, **127**
Sweet Love, **128**
Sweet Words, **129**

T

Tears For You, **130**
Tears Of Love, **131**
That Day Without You, **236**
The Day Of Loneliness, **132**
The End Of The Love Song, **187**
The End, **237**
The First Time, **132**
The Hand Of Time, **133**
The Last Kiss Goodbye, **237**
The Last One I Trust, **134**
The Space Between Us, **188**
The World Doesn't Know, **135**
Those Days, My Love, **188**
Those Happy Days, **135**
To You, With Love, **136**
Today Or Yesterday, **136**
Tomorrow Is Unknown, **137**
Tomorrow When Love Comes, **238**
Tonight, One Last Time, **137**
Tonight, The Last Night, **189**
Too Late To Hold On, **238**

U

Under The Sand, **138**
Until The End, **239**

V

Valentine Day, **139**
Valentine's Loneliness, **140**
Vivid Thoughts, **190**
Voice Of Yesterday, **191**
Voices In The Night, **191**

W

Waiting For Tomorrow, **140**
Waving Goodbye, **141**
What Should I Do?, **142**
When Dreams Come True, **192**
When I Learned That I Loved You, **143**
When Our Love Did Go Wrong, **239**
When Tomorrow Never Comes, **192**
When Will Love Come To Me?, **193**
When You Walked Away, **144**
Where Have You Gone?, **145**
Who Really Knows?, **146**
Who'll Be There When You're Gone?, **194**
Why Do I Love You?, **147**
Wishing Upon The Moon, **148**

Without Knowing, **149**
Words Of Love, **150**
Words Of Pray, **240**
Wrong One To Kiss, **240**
Wrong One To Love, **151**

X

Xena, **195**

Y

Yesterday, Today, Tomorrow, **241**
Yesterday Was A Dream, **242**
You Always Lied To Me, **152**
You Are Gone, **153**
You Are Lost, **153**
You Melt My Heart, **154**
You'll Always Be The One, **243**
Your Love, My Love, **155**
Youth Beauty All Gone, **156**

Z

Zoom My Heart Out, **244**

About The Author

Nghi Nguyen was born in Can Tho, Vietnam, in December of 1983. He moved to the United States in the early 1990s with his family.

In his spare time, Nghi likes to play tennis, read, and write. Beside from poetry, he also writes short stories and screenplays.

He graduated from the University of Maryland University College with a Bachelor in Communication-Journalism, and a Master in Distance Education: Teaching and Training.

Lightning Source UK Ltd.
Milton Keynes UK
UKHW02f0623300718
326485UK00011B/640/P